DRONES

The Professional Drone Pilot's Manual and Drones

(Everything You Need to Know About Building Your Own Quadcopter Drone)

Frank Thomas

Published By Frank Adams

Frank Thomas

All Rights Reserved

Drones: The Professional Drone Pilot's Manual and Drones (Everything You Need to Know About Building Your Own Quadcopter Drone)

ISBN 978-1-77485-403-7

Legal & Disclaimer

The information contained in this book is not designed to replace or take the place of any form of medicine or professional medical advice. The information in this book has been provided for educational and entertainment purposes only.

The information contained in this book has been compiled from sources deemed reliable, and it is accurate to the best of the Author's knowledge; however, the Author cannot guarantee its accuracy and validity and cannot be held liable for any errors or omissions. Changes are periodically made to this book. You must consult your doctor or get professional medical advice before using any of the suggested remedies, techniques, or information in this book.

Upon using the information contained in this book, you agree to hold harmless the Author from and against any damages, costs, and expenses, including any legal fees potentially resulting from the application of any of the information provided by this guide. This

TABLE OF CONTENTS

Part 1

Introduction

Utilizing drones within the modern world is rapidly becoming an integral element of our lives. Nearly all fields, areas and professions are now requiring drones in order to fulfill its duties. The fields of architecture estate management, media and agriculture entertainment and real estate, events management, etc. All have an appreciation for drones. That's not even mentioning the speed at which drones earn enormous profits from the commercial and recreational sales of drones around the world.With this in mind, individuals as well as corporate bodies, investors as well as industries and governments have all started to realize the growing value of purchasing a drone to perform specific tasks. Drones are an air-based Unmanned Aircraft Vehicle which produces excellent images, quality views and videos that are useful to run a business or earn money. It weighs as much as 55 pounds, and is controlled through the Federal Aviation Administration (FAA).Drone enthusiasts who wish to profit from the numerous opportunities offered by the commercial or recreational use of drones should be familiar with the processes and requirements when doing so. They should be aware of what to do with the Drone as well as the restrictions that apply in communicating with Air Traffic Control, understand the way FAA drone regulations operate and learn how to be approved by FAA as well as understand the importance of the classification of airspace and weather in aviation to stay on the safer legal side.In this way the study guide has been designed to provide readers with all the details above and advise those who are preparing to take Part107 of the Part107 Airman Knowledge Test on how to prepare effectively. Additionally, there is some questions that will make applicants ready for the test in a better way.

Chapter 1: How To Obtain A Faa Drone Lizence

A drone license particularly having a Federal Aviation Administration (FAA) drone license, is crucial when operating drones. In the event that your Drone weighs as much as 55 pounds, it's mandated by the FAA to register it and be able for its operation. If you're considering the use of Unmanned Aircraft Vehicles (drones) whether for business or leisure reasons one of the first steps is to make sure they have a FAA-approved drone permit.

What is a DROONE A LICENSE?

Drone licenses are certificate issued by the FAA that permits people to fly or operate drones in a legal manner. It is granted to those who have successfully completed the required of training, test, and certification and have a better understanding of how aviation functions, the specific airspaces that allow drones to fly and the numerous restrictions on drone operation, and how the weather can affect drones' flight, and many more.

To get a drone permit it is necessary to follow these steps

STEP 1:

GET FAA TRACKING NUMBER:

FAA Tracking Number (also known as (FTN) is an unique number that permits an organization like the Federal Aviation Administration to track certified pilots and applicants. Consider it opening an account through the FAA that grants you exclusive access to various facilities and procedures to get certified as drone pilot. This FTN must be requested from you at a later time to be processed further.

STEP 2:

Sign up for training:

Also, you must begin studying the exact method of flying drones, in addition to obtaining an FAA tracker number. This is essential since the process of certification requires the endorsement of a certified instructor that you are able to fly drones. It is not a good idea to pass the FAA drone test without knowing how you can fly drones as this test FAA drone exam will ask to you questions based upon the fundamentals of drone operation.

Step 3:

STUDY:

A step that can't be overlooked is the study aspect of obtaining an drone license. Before you are recognized as being a certified drone pilot you'll have to take a test an exam that you must get a minimum score of 75% to be granted a permit to fly drones. This means that you need to be aware of the areas where questions will be coming out of. Topics such as Aviation Weather, Radio Communications Operations, drone rules loading and performance airspace classification and regulations and so on. These are the elements that make an FAA testing for drones. To obtain a drone permit you must study in order to clear the examination.

Step 4:

DATE OF THE TEST:

After studying, you have to plan the date and time of the test. There are two hours to finish the test, and there are a total of 60 questions to be answered. Select a test location from over 700 certified centers and then check out the FAA test schedule and plan when you will take the test. That's all you must do in this step. For registration for the exam it is necessary to show a government-issued picture ID, like the driver's license or passport. After you've completed the procedure you will be issued an exam number that is 17-digits to keep in your possession for the duration of the exam.

STEP 5:

Take the test:

Understanding key terms, regulations and procedures are essential for taking and passing this FAA drone exam. The test is an opportunity to test your understanding of drone regulations as well as the administration by the FAA. Also, it is to determine whether you have the capability to operate an unmanned aircraft.

Here are some of the requirements to meet prior to you take the test

* You must be at least fifteen or sixteen years old.

* You must be able to write, read and speak using the English language as it is the primary language we utilize throughout the procedure

* You must have a valid way to prove identity like driver's licence or issued by the government, Id card Alien residence card Military ID card, passport, etc.

A Federal Aviation Administration Tracking Number and other information are required at the test centre along with a non-refundable $150 test fee. Be sure to use an official government issued ID. After the test, your results will be announced and posted to the FAA website within 24 hours. If you pass, you are now ready to go to the next step.

Step 6:

Apply for the LICENSE:

If you pass this test, then you need submit a request to your certificate from the Federal Aviation Administration by completing the 8710-13 form on the IACRA website to obtain the remote pilot certificate and become certified to operate drones. It is located beneath "Start new Application." Choose "Pilot," and under Certifications, choose "Remote Pilot," then "Other Path Information," and finally "Start Application." When you have completed the form an investigation into your background will be conducted, and temporary licenses will be sent to you via email first , before the permanent license is issued via normal mail in 120 days. The license for permanent use is renewed every year for a period of 24 months.

Chapter 2: What Do People Want Their Phone Licenses For?

There are a myriad of avenues where a drone can help. It can be used for recreational or commercial reasons, photography or videography or for industries and social media or even agriculture These platforms and many more will require that anyone who wants to make use of them must possess an authorization for drones.

You may be wondering whether the long and arduous process of getting a licence in order to fly and operate a drone worth the effort. It is true that certified drone pilots can utilize their licenses for a variety of activities to earn money and offer employment opportunities. The process can be quite complicated, but it's definitely worth it due to the benefits in the end. Here are the things people use their drone licenses to do.

1. to make money:

The current state of the economy as is currently and in our time favors the industry of information and technology where the usage of drones is a part. There is a growing need for certified drone pilots and the opportunities are endless because of the quality results they bring to videography and photography. Additionally the side, a drone pilot who is certified could earn up to $200 an hour, and earn between $30,000 and $85,000 per year , or more, based on the pilot's experience. To be able to make use of drones commercial use, you need to possess a drone licence.

There are many avenues to earn money include teaching others how to fly drones or using social media sites such as YouTube advertising and promotions such as roof and site inspections and real estate photography Wedding and special event photography as well as emergency and public service drones, aerial surveying, mapping, selling stock images as well as videos on the internet, among others.

2. To fly in CERTAIN Airspaces WITHOUT RESERVATION:

Certified drone pilots are legally entitled to the permission to fly drones in certain airspaces with no restrictions. The certificate issued to them by the Federal Aviation Administration means that they possess the required skill and experience, as well as having the necessary knowledge of what is to fly drones. A drone permit allows the drone pilot to display his certificate to fly in specific zones.

3. TO GET JOB OFFERS:

Certain drone-related jobs and clients would prefer that their drone pilot be licensed to fly or operate an Unmanned Aircraft Vehicle before offering the job. The reason is that the drone's license legally permits the pilot to fly drones. Certain industries and businesses employ drone pilots who are certified as employees in-house because they have the necessary skills and knowledge and is certified to fly drones.

4. For SELF-EMPLOYMENT:

Drone pilots have everything they need to be self-employed. In addition to earning a profit from home drone pilots could build a substantial customer base, and then become professional with an official drone permit. The drone license allows them to be classified as professional drone pilots in the field, and they are able to benefit from that full-time.

5. To reduce the risk of FINES and RISKS:

A drone license indicates that you've got the legal authority for operating a drone in specific airspaces, and for whatever reason is permitted by law. Anyone who is not certified may be charged with a fine and even arrested since the drone is not operating with the necessary license. This is the reason that most drone pilots are certified in order to lower the chance of being fined or taken into custody. The FAA has a stricter policy for drone operators who operate commercially with no drone license.

6. To become a better and SAFER DRONE PILOT

The process of becoming certified and passing Part 107 drone tests and getting certified Part 107 drone test can increase the understanding of the subject to help the pilot become more competent and equipped to fly the drone. The course teaches drone pilots how to stay safe in the air and what warning signs to look for, the best height the drone can fly and what to do in the event of an emergency and what regulations govern drones' operations. A drone pilot certified by the FAA has the necessary knowledge about the process of being certified. This means he is better prepared to fly drones.

Chapter 3: What Can I Earn With An Faa Drone License?

A myriad of doubts and questions may be lingering in the minds of potential pilots of small aircrafts that are unmanned. Think about whether it's worthwhile to obtain an Federal Aviation Administration license and becoming a commercial pilot or whether it's a profitable business idea. If one decides to go into earning money through drones for commercial purposes and drones, not to mention.

The current tide of wealth of now and into our time favors the industry of information and technology where the usage of drones is a part. There is a growing demand for drone pilots who are certified and there are plenty of opportunities due to the quality outcomes they can bring to videography and photography. As a side note the drone pilot could earn as much as $200 per hour, and can even earn an annual salary of $30,000-85,000 or greater.

READ THESE INDICES:

Drone pilots are in High Demand:

The Information and Technology Industry is in a stage where there is a growing demand for online content and through social media platforms. In addition, there is the film and entertainment business and events that require drones. Certified drone pilots can profit from this potential.

Low Start Cost:

Commercial drones do not cost a lot. The process of getting a drone registered is not costly or laborious. In comparison to the money the drone pilot earns it is likely that the process of creating his own drone business will not be expensive. It will include the Drone as well as batteries for additional drones for the camera, video and photo editing software, as well as the FAA license.

Self-Employment:

Drone pilots can do all they need to be self-employed. In addition to earning a profit by doing side work drone pilots could also have an extensive client base and later become professional by obtaining their drone licence.

Earning money through the use of your drone is your decision. You decide what you charge customers as well as the amount you charge per hour, and also the types of jobs you will take on. Here are some ways you can earn money from your Drone.

REAL ESTATE PHOTOGRAPHY AS WELL AS VIDEOGRAPHY:

The real estate industry offers huge possibilities to drone pilots. A majority of the work performed on-site requires the use of an aerial view, which will enhance the work being done. Certain structures are better portrayed using drones, which is the reason why drone pilots is able to leverage real estate in order to earn profits.

Roof Inspection:

As well as the real estate industry, drones can also be employed to look over areas that are difficult or costly to reach. For instance, insurance companies prefer using drones to look at the roof of their buildings since it is less expensive than sending an employee to inspect the roof in their place. The job can be done quickly and simple for drone pilots and can be a new method to earn money.

SELL DRONE PHOTOS VIDEOS:

A drone pilot may make use of the quality of his drone photos regardless of whether they are videos or photos and sell them online. Professional photographers can access an online marketplace where they sell their stock images and videos. Drone pilots can take advantage of the opportunity to offer high-quality video and photos through his Drone. Websites such as Shutterstock, iStock, and Adobe stock provide this service.

AERIAL SURVEYING and MAPPING:

Another method of earning money as a drone pilot by doing aerial surveys and mapping. A drone equipped with a high-resolution camera is able to fly over a certain terrain to capture photographs of the area and then stitch them together to make a map using the software. The images taken of drone Drone could be utilized to make 3D models. Drone pilots can profit from this field to earn money.

WEDDING COVERAGE FOR EVENTS AND WEDDINGS:

The most popular avenues to earn money as a drone pilot is wedding and event coverage. Professional photographers or videographers who wants to add more high-end to their business may also obtain drone. The aerial shots taken by drones at events and weddings could be distinctive and high-quality that is the reason why event planners often ask specific drone pilots. Another method of earning money as drone pilots.

Public and Emergency Services:

Public agencies such as the fire department and police have seen an increase in the use of drones as well as drone pilots through the decades. They use drones to aid in missions of search and rescue and inspections, surveillance, and much more. Sometimes, they employ drone pilots and other professionals to help them achieve their mission while paying them.

Inspection of the agricultural product:

Drones also play a vital role in the assessment of vast farms and are used to detect of diseases in plants, pests as well as monitoring the operation. Making detailed photos of them could be extremely beneficial in modern farming. Drone pilots are able to be actively engaged in this endeavor and take advantage of the chance to earn money.

Other options include instructing others on how to fly drones, using social media platforms like YouTube as well as advertising and promotions, and so on.

Chapter 4: What Do You Bring To The Airman Test Of Knowledge?

If you are using it for recreational or commercial purpose the process of becoming a drone pilot is only possible if you are licensed to fly drones. It is the Airman Knowledge Test is required to become a certified drone pilot. It also grants the privilege the ability to pilot drones. The test center will typically give you a test supplement books, blank paper pencil, transparent sheet as well as a dry eraser markers.

REQUIREMENTS FOR TEST TAKEN:

Here are some of the requirements to meet prior to you take the test

* Must be between the age of 15-16 years old

* Must be able write, read, and speak using the English language as it is the language that we utilize throughout the procedure

* Must possess a valid method of identification, like a driver's license or a official government issued Id card Alien resident card Military ID card, passport, etc.

* Get an confirmation from an authorized trainer, stating that you have taken a an in-person or at-home study course and have the necessary preparation to take the exam.

Apart from armed with the necessary knowledge, terminology and details regarding how to pass the FAA test, when you go to the testing location, it is important to be aware of a few aspects that an aspiring unmanned aircraft pilot should be prepared with. These comprise:

Important Documents:

Certain documents are required you have to bring along. They are mostly used to establish your identification and to prove that you are a legal citizen. The documents could differ depending on the status of your citizenship.

A) UNITED STATES CITIZEN AND RESIDENT INFANTS:

This means that you must be armed with a U.S. driver's license, U.S. Military ID, Passport or Alien Residency Card, or Government Issued ID Card. This is necessary to prove your identity. It is important to note that you don't need to carry every one of these cards is essential. You may choose to stick with the ones you already have. The identity document must also include the name of the person applying, his middle name, photo as well as the date of birth, address, signature and address.

B) Non-UNITED State Citizens:

Anyone who is not a citizen from this country in the United States can go with their passport, government-issued I.D.

card or the U.S. driver's license. It is a government issued I.D. card is issued by any government entity. The ID card should also include the name of the person applying, his middle name, photo as well as the date of birth, address and signature.

C) TEST AUTHORIZATION

There are specific documents such as an endorsement by a licensed or certified instructor, which you are required to bring for the airman knowledge test. This endorsement could differ based on the airman test you're preparing for. The endorsement should also contain the photograph and name of the potential drone pilot along with the phrases "the applicant is ready to take the airman knowledge test."

Retaker candidates must also submit a separate certification from an instructor certified by the FAA that outlines the percentage level of test score as well as whether applicants have met the FAA requirements for writing the test.

d) ATTESTATION:

This is only for people younger than 18 years old and does not provide any form for identification. They must be accompanied by an adult or parent to verify their identity. They must also bring an official diploma of completion, certificate of accomplishment, a written statement and logbook entries.

1. TOOLS:

Alongside documents, you'll also be required to bring specific tools that will aid in your writing skills for the test. The tools include

a) Protractor

B) Plotter

C) A magnifier (for tiny icons and words). There was a report that some terms and icons were difficult to view with the eyes. This is the reason why magnifiers is very useful.

d) A standard Calculator (an advanced calculator is not accepted)

2. It is also required that you be able to pay $150. This is the fee required to write your Airman Knowledge test.

In addition to the items mentioned above it is not necessary to bring any other sheets, documents or documents. If you fail to adhere, other items will not be accepted to be used during the test.

Chapter 5: Registration Of Drones

Vs. A Drone Certification

This chapter will provide you with all the necessary information on Drone identification and registration. The two processes are as vital, however with distinct distinctions. Drone registration is the registration directly of a small, unmanned vehicle and drone certification is the necessary license in order to use the Drone. While drone registration is applicable to the Drone as a whole drone, drone certification is applicable on the drone's pilot.

To be able to clearly comprehend the differences It is crucial to understand the process involved.

DROONE REGISTRATION

The Federal Aviation Administration FAA has stated that all unmanned aircraft vehicles need to be registered, except for those weighing less than 250g. If your Drone weighs more than 250g, you need to register it.

HOW DO I REGISTER?

Registration Information:

1. Then you will have for your physical address as well as a the address for your mail

2. Your telephone number and e-mail address

3. The model and type of your Drone

4. The unique number of identification that is are on the back of your Drone and the serial number

5. Additionally, you will be required to bring a debit or credit card to make registration and payment.

Registration Costs:

1. You'll be required to pay $5 to purchase the drone. The registration will be valid for 3 years.

2. The registration for recreational Drone use Drone per Drone costs $5. is valid for 3 years.

3. Drone registrations is not transferable from one user or owner to another. This will be stated when payment is completed.

Conditions to Register a Drone:

1. The applicant must be 13 years old or older. If the drone's owner is younger than 13, an individual aged 13 years old or more must be registered to own the Drone. This could be parents or guardians.

2. The applicant must be an United States citizen.

3. The drones of foreign operators are likely to be issued an ownership certificate instead of a certificate of registration. The FAA recognizes the certificate issued to a pilot from a country other than the one who registers a drone as a document of ownership.

Drone registration is possible on the FAA website, as well as via post. After completing your registration you will be issued an FAA-issued registration certificate which means that the FAA recognizes your Drone. It is mandatory to carry your registration certificate on hand whenever you fly your Drone.

Furthermore it is required to label or mark your Drone with your registration number prior to beginning to fly the drone. Agents of law enforcement are able to request drone owners or pilots to disclose details about their drone registration as deemed acceptable from the Federal Aviation Administration (FAA).

Drone CERTIFICATION

The FAA requires pilots with Unmanned Aircraft Vehicles with a weight less than 55 pounds, to be licensed as drones prior to operating the Drone to be used for recreation or for commercial purposes. There are steps and procedures in obtaining a drone certificate.

1. Know the Rules Know the Rules: The FAA has a variety of rules which govern the use drones. Certain restrictions, waivers controlled and uncontrolled

airspaces that allow drone pilots to fly drones and other drones. are to be adhered to. The drone pilot must be aware of these regulations before he is able to start to work towards drone certification.

2. Take The Knowledge Test: understanding key concepts, rules and procedures is the key for getting through this FAA drone examination. The test is an opportunity to test your understanding of drone regulations as well as the administration by the FAA. Also, it will determine whether you possess the technical capability to manage unmanned aircraft vehicles. It is essential that the candidate take time to study for the test. The Drone test is $150.

Here are some guidelines to follow prior to you take the exam

* You must be at least fifteen or sixteen years old.

* You must be able to write, read and speak within the English language as it is the language that we utilize throughout the entire procedure

* You must possess a valid way to prove identity like a driver's license or official government issued Id card Alien residence card Military ID card, passport, etc.

* You must have an confirmation from an authorized trainer, stating that you have taken a the ground training or home study course and have the necessary preparation to take the exam.

* Be in a steady physical and mental state to fly drones.

After passing the test, you fill out the FAA complete form available on their site

3. Make sure you register your drone:

Your Drone is also required to be registered prior to you begin using it. This is accomplished by providing specific information regarding the Drone and then paying the fee of $5 to register it.

Chapter 6: Preparing For Faa Droone Test

This Federal Aviation Administration drone test will require applicants to be aware of FAA rules such as terms, weather and aircraft operations regulations, airspace regulations loading, performance etc. The test taker has to score 70% in order to pass the test and the preparation for the test requires a lot of study. To help you prepare, this chapter will focus on a few aspects to be focused on.

AREAS TO DISCUSS:

1. REGULATIONS ABOUT AIRSPACE AND CLASSIFICATION

Knowing about airspace, its rules and classifications is crucial. They inform the person applying of the restrictions within the airspace accessible to flying drones, as well as the operation and technical aspects involved, the communication structures, Air Traffic Control, and the extent to the drone is able to be controlled.

Additionally, it will give the airspace types classification, such as the controlled and uncontrolled classifications, and will provide a thorough analysis of the airspace that is available for drones. The section covers 15 to 25 percent of the questions on the test.

2. AVISION WEATHER:

The applicant must also be aware of aviation weather conditions. The weather conditions determine whether flying an unmanned aircraft is feasible or not. Information on wind, visibility temperatures, wind speed, etc. In this section, you will be able to provide information on the tools used in collecting weather data (METAR as well as PIREPS) as well as the different agencies responsible for aviation weather, as well as the importance of adhering to the data in the weather report and their analysis. This section comprises approximately 11-15% of exam questions.

3. Performance and loading:

Another crucial aspect to consider when preparing is understanding how performance and loading work. To comprehend how loading impacts drone performance, it is important to know the amount of weight needed for takeoff as well as the height and the maximum limits. This allows the drone pilot understand the basics of drone operation, maintenance and flight. You should study this topic to pass the drone test as it is about 7-11% of the test questions.

4. Radio Communication Procedures:

It is also crucial to understand how radio communications function and how aircraft communicate with Air Traffic Control (ATC) stations, and the reasons it is essential for aviation. There are situations where the drone operator must be in contact with an Air Traffic Control (ATC) station. For instance flying a drone at the vicinity of an airport or within an airport requires approval and proper communication with Air Traffic Control. This is the reason you should be aware of this during your preparation for the test on drones. This area is about 35-45 percent of the test questions.

5. Drone REGULATIONS:

Understanding drone regulations is essential. In this section, you will learn Part 107 generally, requirements of obtaining a drone licence and the requirements to fly your Drone and drone license application procedure and what you need to carry to carry with you when operating the Drone. These regulations are crucial to the prospective applicant and the questions will be based on these regulations for the exam. This is about 15-45 percent of the drone testing.

Other sub-topics and topics include the following topics:

1. Regulations and Limitations on the flight operations.

2. Airspace regulations and types of airspace that govern drone operations.

3. Understanding of weather conditions in relation to drones.

4. Drone loading and operation.

5. Control and administration of the crew.

6. Emergency management.

7. Aeronautical decision-making.

8. Airport operation.

9. Preflight inspection.

10. Drugs' effects.

11. Aircraft behavior.

It is vital to learn these subjects in order for passing the test in a comprehensive manner.

Chapter 7: Federal Administration

For Aviation Test Acronyms

Drone operations, regardless of whether they are for commercial or recreational purposes is a requirement for the understanding or understanding of words that are acronyms, words, and diction that are related to or necessary for the domain that is the Federal Aviation Administration. In this context, that people who prepare for the FAA Drone Test must familiarize them with these words.

You are already aware that an acronym can refer to abbreviations that have been taken from the first letters of words to create an additional word. This is an alphabetical list of acronyms that are specific to the testing and use of drones. These include, but aren't restricted to:

1. A/C Aircraft
2. AA: Anti-aircraft
3. AAA: Anti-aircraft artillery
4. AAIB: Air Accidents Investigation Board
5. AAM: Air-to-air missile
6. AAV: Autonomous Air Vehicle
7. Aviation Block Infrastructure: Aviation Block Infrastructure
8. The ADM Air Defense Missiles
9. Air District Offices: Air District Offices
10. The AIM is: Aeronautical Information Manual
11. AIS (automated identification system)
12. ASOS: Automated Surface Observing Systems
13. ATC Air Traffic Control
14. The AWC Aviation Weather Center
15. AWOS: Automated Weather Watching Systems

16. COW A Certificate of Waiver

17. CFIT Controlled flight in Terrain

18. CTAF: The Common Traffic Advisory Frequency

19. CRM: Crew Resource Management

20. Control Station: CS Station

21. Danger Area: Danger Zone

22. DARO: Defense Airborne Reconnaissance Office

23. DARPAis the acronym for Defense Advanced Research Projects Agency

24. DAS: Detection of Acoustical Signature

25. DCPA Distance between vessels that approach CPA

26. DDoS: Distributed Denial of Service cyber attack

27. The DFCS is the Digital Flight Control System

28. The DLI is the Data Link Interface. Data Link Interface

29. DOS: Denial of Service cyber attack

30. D-R-O-N: Direct, Report, Observe, Notify & Execute

31. ECM Electromagnetic compatibility

32. ECR: Electronic combat reconnaissance

33. EDC Estimated Date of completion

34. EDEW: The Effects on Directed Energy Weapons

35. EEZP"EXP" is an acronym for Exclusive Economic Zone security

36. The ELT is an emergency locator transmitter.

37. EMR: Electromagnetic Radiation

38. ESM: Electromagnetic Spectrum

39. EO: Electro-optical (sensing)

40. The EOTS system is an electro-optical targeting system.

41. ERPJ Power radiated effective of the jammer

42. ERPS: Effective radiated energy of the signal transmitter you want to use

43. Electronic Signal Monitoring: ESM.

44. FAA: Federal Aviation Administration

45. AR: False Alarm Rates

46. FCC: Federal Communications Commission

47. FRD: Fixed Radial Distance

48. The FSDO is the Flight Standard District Office

49. The FSS is the acronym for Flight Service Station. Flight Service Station

50. GBU Guided Bomb Unit

51. GCS: Ground Control Station

52. GDPR: General Data Protection Regulation

53. GDT: Ground data terminal

54. GEO Geostationary Satellite orbiting Earth

55. GNS: Global Navigation Satellite System

56. GPWS (Ground proximity warning system)

57. GTA: Ground -to -Air Defense

58. GPS: Global Position System

59. HAE High Altitude Endurance

60. HAPS High Altitude Platforms

61. HEAT: High-explosive warhead for anti-tank

62. HELWS High Energy Laser Weapon system

63. HMI: Human machine interface

64. HPL High Power Laser Weapon

65. HPM: High-powered microwave defense

66. HVT: High Value Target

67. LOC The location of the accident

68. MAD magnetic anomaly detection

69. MADIS Marine Air Defense Integrated System

70. MAE: Medium-altitude endurance

71. MAGTF Marine ground task force

72. MALDRONE: Malware is injected into the critical SAA to create UAS

73. MAST: Measurement and Signal Intelligence

74. MATS: Mobile Aircraft Tracking System

75. M-AUDS: Mobile Anti-UAV Defense System

76. MAV Micro-air vehicle

77. MCE: Mission Control Elements

78. MDR: Missed Rates of Detection

79. MEMS: Micro-electromechanical systems

80. MEO: Medium Earth Orbit satellite

81. MGTOW: Maximum gross takeoff weight

82. METAR Meteorological Terminal Air Report

83. MSL: Mean Sea Level

84. NAC Network Access Control

85. The NACA is the National Advisory Committee on Aeronautics

86. NASA: National Aeronautics and Space Administration

87. NASAMS: National Advanced Surface to Air Missile System

88. NAV Nano-air vehicle

89. NBC Chemical, biological and chemical conflict

90. NCW: Network Centric Warfare

91. NEC: Network-enabled capability

92. The NIEM: National Information Exchange Model

93. The NTSB National Transportation Safety Board

94. The NWS National Weather Service

95. OIO: Offensive Information Operations

96. OPA Optionally piloted aircraft

97. Optionally piloted air vehicle

98. OPSEC: Operations Security

99. OSI: Open Systems Interconnection

100. PAVE The Pilot Airplane Environmental pressure External

101. PHOTINT Photographic Intelligence

102. PIC"Pilot in Command

103. PIT Proximity Traffic of Intruders

104. ALC or Programmable Logic Controllers

105. POS System for Position and Orientation System

106. PreACT = Partnership for Regional East Africa Counterterrorism (PREACT)

107. PRF: Pulse Repetition Frequency codes

108. PRM = Precision Runway Monitor

109. PSD: Power Spectral Density

110. PSR = Primary Surveillance Radar

111. RAC: Range air controller

112. The term RADAR means Radio Detection and Ranging

113. RADINT: Radar intelligence

114. RCE: Remote Code Execution

115. RCO Remote-control operator

116. RED: Risk Estimate Distance

117. RF: Radio Frequency

118. The RGB is Red Green Blue for the VIS camera

119. RGT: Remote Ground Terminal

120. The Route Manual for RM

121. Remote Pilot In Command

122. SAFO Warning to Safety for Operators

123. SIDA SIDA: Security Identification Display Area

124. SUAS: Small Unmanned Aircraft System

125. SRM: Single-Pilot Resource Management

126. TAF Area Forecast: Terminal Area Forecast

127. TFR Temporary Flight Restrictions

128. TM Tracking Traffic

129. UAS = Unmanned Aircraft System

130. UNCOM: Universal Integrated Community

131. UTC = Universal Coordinated Time

132. VFR Visual Flight Rules

133. VLOS: Visual Line of Sight

134. W&B (Wood and Balance) (Aircraft)

Chapter 8: Significant Part107

Aviation Terms

Apart from understanding terms and acronyms, the drone pilot should be aware of the various terms used in aviation which are crucial. These terms will give the drone owner insight into how flying and aviation drones function. The user will be aware of the way drones operate in accordance with their Federal Aviation Administration standard.

Part 107 drones can also be known as Unmanned Aircraft Systems (UAS) in spite of their use in commercial or recreational for recreational or commercial. The definitions and terms below (in not in any particular order) relate to aviation and drones, as interpreted in authorities of the United States Government.

DRONE:

The term refers to any type of aircraft built or designed to operate or be operated remotely, without any human pilot or direct human intervention inside the aircraft. Drones can be controlled externally.

FAA:

FAA is the acronym as the Federal Aviation Administration; it is an agency and part of the United States Government responsible for the regulation and control of activities of public aviation across the United States. They test, register the air traffic, and issue certificates for civil and public aviation within the United States.

CONTROLLER:

The Controller is the device used to interface with users which is used to control the flight of drones. It is known in the form of the Control Station (CS). It is also said as software that is used on mobile phones, or electronic devices to control the drone's flight.

AUGROUND LEVEL:

Above Ground Level refers to the level at which drones are at. One of the permissible permissions to the altitude drones' operation according to the FAA and the FAA, is a ceiling of 400 feet, which can be (121.9 meters) over a structure. This means that the drone user is able to fly the Drone up to a height of 400 feet based on the structure they are flying over.

AIRMAN:

In this sense, an airman is a person regardless of gender who is recognized through the FAA for flying a drone or carry out similar tasks. The person who is certified that they have fulfilled the requirements prior to the operation and use of drones.

GEOGRAPHIC INFORMATION SYSTEM (GIS):

It is a method that is used to collect, analyze storage, manage and display the location of data. It records the geographical information captured by the drone's sensor.

GPS (GLOBAL POSITIONING System):

GPS is a term used to describe an directional satellite radio or navigational system utilized to find any spot on the earth. Signals are broadcast by multiple satellites. Communication is carried out through the navigational receptors on the Drone to relay information on the location of.

Part of 107:

Part107 refers to a description of the section of the United States Code of Federal Regulations (14 USC Part 107) which regulates commercial smaller drones. They weigh less than (25 kilograms). In another way, Part 107 is a part in the Code of Regulations which regulates how small drones are used commercially, particularly ones that are less weighty than.

SUBMANNED AIRCRAFT System (sUAS):

sUAS is a term used to describe the unmanned aircraft system (Drone) which weighs just under 25 kilograms (55 pounds). In accordance with the FAA the aircraft that are less than this weight are able to be used commercially in accordance with part 107 of its rules.

PERSON in charge of the controls:

A second person, apart from that of the drone's remote pilot who controls the flight for the tiny Unmanned aircraft system (sUAS) however under close supervision by that drone's pilot. According to the Part 107 regulations, the FAA stipulates that drone controllers do not have to get an authorization for commercial use.

PITCH:

Pitch refers to the direction of movement on the Drone or any other traditional Aircraft either upwards or downwards.

TFR (TEMPORARY FLIGHT RESTRICTION):

This is an interim FAA limitation on flight actions within a particular area and in a certain height.

WAIVER:

Waiver refers to a waiver granted by the FAA which grants an aviation controller authority to disregard certain rules or guidelines which govern the operation of the aircraft. This is because the waiver permits the operator of the aircraft to operate in violation of specific rules or guidelines established in accordance with the FAA.

NOTAM (NOTICE to Airmen):

Notice to airmen is any announcement or published report issued by the FAA which informs airmen or aircraft operators about any conditions or changes at the airport, or warning of any aspect or system of airspace which could interfere with the flow of flight. For drones or sUASs A notice to airmen may contain an indefinite restriction on flight due to modifications to any aspect of the airspace system. Drone operators should be aware of the NOTAM very seriously.

LITHIUM-ION (LION) BATTERY:

Lithium-Ion battery is the type rechargeable battery made of lithium compounds. This kind of battery is used primarily to power small airplanes that are not piloted. systems.

Chapter 9: Key Part Of 107 Terms
And Phrases

Along with knowing important aviation terms, anyone who is preparing to take taking the Part 107 test must also be aware of the key words and phrases that go along to the part 107 drone exam. Certain of these terms refer to drone regulations and concepts that provide a brief overview of what the pilot must be aware of prior to conducting the test, or before attempting to obtain certification to fly and own drones.

Here is a list of the most important terms and phrases from part 107:

The Aeronautical Knowledge Test The aeronautical test is intended to assess the skills that a pilot has. This is an exam similar to a driver's license , or a certification test. It covers specific aspects connected to the operation of drones and management, drone parts as well as emergency procedure. The test is accessible for those who are over 14 years of age. But, after the test has been completed only those who are aged 16 or older can receive the certificate. So, those who pass the aeronautical knowledge test when they are 14 must wait until 16 years old before receiving either a license or certificate.

UAV License It is a UAV license refers to an Unmanned Aircraft Vehicle operator certificate. UAV is generally known as drone, and this implies it is a drone. UAV certificate is actually a certificate granted to UAV operators to allow them to use their drone's use. After you've completed a part 107 exam or test and passed the test, the next thing you need to do is to apply for an UAV license, which is a permanent license to use commercially drones. The UAV license is valid for six weeks to be granted.

Small Operator Certificate for sUAS: SUAS means small unmanned aircraft, which can also refer to drones that weigh less than 55 pounds. Small operator certificates for sUAS are an unmanned aviation vehicle (UAV) certificate or license issued to the UAV operator that permits the operator legally to use the Unmanned Aircraft Vehicle with a weight less than 55 pounds. It could also be referred to as an pilot's licence for small aircrafts.

14 CFR Part 16 is a formula written to obtain private certification for pilots. The CFR is the acronym for Code of Federal Regulation. Pilots who wish to be trained in part 16 of the 14. CFR part 16 guidelines

should be ready to undergo instruction that requires skills and knowledge. The certification permits the pilot to operate drones for commercial purposes. With Part 107 certification, you can fly drones commercially. Part 107 certification, you don't require an 14CFR Part 16 certification.

NPRM (NOTICE of proposed regulation) A common term that is used frequently in the Small Unmanned Aircraft systems world is the NPRM. It is an 195-page document that acts as a notice that outlines arrangements that are intended to alter the regulations for commercialization of tiny, unmanned aircraft. After the NPRM was released in February of 2015, the public started to comprehend the new drone regulations and rules set by the FAA through the NPRM. However the NPRM has been removed from use due to the publication part 107. Part 107.

BLOS (BEYOND the line of sight) Certification The act of operating or flying unmanned aircraft requires operators to keep a clear line of sight. Beyond that line indicates that the aircraft unmanned is out of the sight of the pilot. This is a certification given by commercial drone pilots who find it difficult to operate within a visible line of sight. Part 107 contains a clause that permits users to request an beyond-the-line-of-sight certificate. After this certificate is granted they are able to fly drones over individuals and fly drones in the night.

Visual Line of Sight (VLOS) is operating the Unmanned Aircraft within the visible area that the pilot is in. Contrary to BLOS (Beyond Line of Sight) Unmanned aircraft can't fly over humans and can't fly the Drone at night.

NOTAM (NOTICE to Airmen) Note to airmen is any type of announcement or publication by the FAA that informs airmen and aircraft operators regarding any conditions or changes at an airport, as well as warning of any aspect that is part of an airspace system which could impact the operation of the flight. For drones and sUAS the notice to airmen could be an interim restriction to flying due to changes in any element of an airspace system. Drone operators need to be aware of NOTAM.

Above Ground Level Above Ground Level signifies the highest point that a drone is flying. One of the permissible permissions to the altitude drone's use as per the FAA and the FAA, is a ceiling of 400 feet which can be (121.9 meters) over a structure. This means that the drone user is able to fly the Drone up to a maximum of 400 feet, based on the structure that he is flying over.

Chapter 10: Part 107 Operational Limitations

Part 107 contains a restriction on the use of drones in accordance with the FAA. These restrictions on operation are intended to stop accidents and fraudulent drone use by drone pilots and drone operators. In the Code of Federal Regulations has specific regulations and rules that govern the operation of drones. Some of the restrictions on operations are:

No OPERATION within or near airports:

There are restrictions on operations of smaller Unmanned Aircraft systems within certain airspaces, and one such airspaces is the airport. A drone pilot or pilot is permitted in flying drones, or operating drones close to airports without air traffic control approval that permits him to do this. This restriction is outlined in Section 41, the Part 107 operations.

No OPERATION from a vehicle in MOTION:

Another limitation to operation for pilots of unmanned aircraft is the limitation on operating floating drowns from an aircraft or vehicle that is moving. It is extremely difficult or unpractical to control drones while driving or aircraft with no prior planning, which is the reason it is a restriction on operation. It is however permitted in areas that have a low or limited population.

FLY IN VISUAL LINE OF SIGHT:

Unmanned Aircraft Vehicles are to be controlled and flown in the direct line of view of either the operator or pilot. The law requires under section 31 to have all aircrafts without pilots operate by pilots who do not have the use of corrective lensesor aiding devices such as binoculars, and be within the range of view for the pilot. In practical terms, this means that the pilot can't operate the aircraft beyond one thousand 5 hundred yards (1,500) that of the pilot until it is unobservable to the pilot's eyes.

OPERATIONS OVER people:

Drones flying over people is a different limitation of operating drones that are not piloted by aircraft. This ban prohibits the use of drones in large groups of people. It makes sure that the people are at the safest distance in the event of an accident, to avoid the Drone hitting them. Except for those directly working with the Drone The drone's operators should not fly drones directly over the people.

Hazardous Materials:

Small unmanned aircraft aren't allowed to fly while transporting harmful materials or content. Materials that pose a risk are those or objects that cause harm or may cause harm to the health of the public as well as property when transported commercially, mostly by using small aircrafts that are not piloted.

Flying at night:

Another limitation to flying drones that are not piloted is the restriction on flying drones at night. Although pilots are instructed to fly within a clear line of sight but flying drones during the night could be in violation of this rule.

Flying without a visual obstructor:

Visual observer (VO) is a person that remote pilots assign to help the pilot, as well as the person who controls the drone that is not manned. The restriction stipulates that pilots and operators of small aircrafts that are unmanned cannot fly drones without a visible observer. This is as there has to be a clear visual communication between both participants during the flight control.

AREA RESTRUCTIONS:

Recreational drones are banned or restricted in certain airspaces. In addition to limiting the distance of 8 km near airports, drones that are used for recreation are restricted from military bases and facilities including stadiums, national parks and all other airspace subject to FAA limitations.

AVOID ALL OTHER AIRCRAFTS:

There is also a way to see and avoid the limitations on small aircrafts that are not piloted. Drone operators are required to comply with air traffic control regulations , by not circling other drones flying in the air.

REGISTRATION Requirements:

Before pilots are able to operate a small, unmanned aircraft vehicle, the pilot has to be able to prove their qualifications certification, waiver, and license that has been certified and verified through the FAA. A certificate similar to UAV (Unmanned Aircraft Vehicle) licenses are mandatory.

Above Ground Level:

Above Ground Level is the level that a drone is at. One of the permits allowed for the altitude drone's use according to the FAA which is a maximum of 400 feet which can be (121.9 meters) over a structure.

The user is able to fly the Drone to a height of 400 feet based on the structure they are flying over.

MARIJUANA OR DRUG RESERVATION:

Apart from the dangers drone operators aren't permitted to transport drugs or marijuana in any way regardless of whether it is legal allowed that the driver consume these substances or not. They must ensure that their unmanned vehicles aren't in their use as a vehicle to transport drugs or marijuana.

Chapter 11: Airspace Classification

Airspace Classification refers to the complicated design of the navigational device that regulates and defines what is allowed to fly in particular areas and areas. Before a drone pilot operator takes off with an aircraft, or a Small Unmanned Aircraft Vehicle, they must be aware of the various types of airspaces in order to ensure an appropriate and safe flight. There are airspaces that are regulated restricted airspaces, airspaces with prohibited use, and restricted airspaces, and others.

REGULATORY (CONTROLLED AIRSPACE):

Controlled airspace is a major concern for Unmanned Aircraft Vehicles (UAV) operators. Controlled airspace has three dimensions and pilots must be aware of the airspace they are planning to fly within. As per the (ICAO) International Civil Aviation Organization there are several classified airspaces that are controlled between Class A and G. However, while the Federal Aviation Administration (FAA) recognizes classes A,B C, D, C, G, and E. However, since Class G is not recognized by the FAA. but Class F is not recognized as a valid classification by the FAA.

Class A:

The FAA stipulates that the highest point that an unmanned vehicle can fly is within 400 feet of the ground (AGL). However Class A airspace is required to be maintained at an elevation of 18,000 feet of Mean Sea Level (MSL) up to 600 feet flight level (FL) which includes airspace that covers waters of the 12-nautical miles

(NM) from the coastline of the 48 states that are adjacent and Alaska. Only with approval from the FAA can drones be used in violation of this classification. The operators who operate Small Unmanned Aircraft Systems cannot be operating in the airspace of this classification without a specific authorization.

Class B:

This class requires that flights be between the surface and 10,000 feet of MSL (Mean Sea Level) across the airports that are the busiest to operate airports. This zone requires that ATC (Air Traffic Control) issues approval and clearance for flights operating in Airspace Class B. Unless they are approved by the ATC the aircraft vehicles are required to be equipped with a two-way radio that can communicate to Air Traffic Control on the appropriate frequencies in Airspace of Class B. Users who operate Small Unmanned Aircraft Systems cannot operate in this airspace without obtaining specific approvals.

Class C:

This airspace states that the flight must be conducted from the surface up to 4000 feet above the elevation of the airport and adjacent airports that have an operating control tower which is served by an approach control using radar, and that they must be able to accommodate a certain amount of IFR (Instrument Flight Rules) passengers enplanements or operations. Class C airspace Class C airspace has more frequent as Class B airspace, which requires communications between aircrafts and Air Traffic Control. The operators who operate Small Unmanned Aircraft Systems cannot operate within this airspace without prior authorization.

Class D:

Airspace that extends from the surface to 2,500 feet higher than the airport's elevation, and the surrounding airports that have a control tower in operation. To operate in Class D airspace the pilot has to be authorized by ATC (Air Traffic Control). The operators who operate Small Unmanned Aircraft Systems cannot operate in this airspace unless they have the authorization of ATC.

Class E:

The airspace in question is not classed as a separate entity from the other (A B, C, D). Class E airspace encompasses many airspaces in the United States, providing enough airspace to ensure safe control of aircraft and instruments for Flight Rules management. Class E airspace can include more than one set of flying heights. In certain areas 14,500 feet is sea level, while 1,200 feet is the ground in other locations as well as Flight Line 600 feet in certain other locations. Airspace in Class E does not extend beyond 18,000 feet. Users in Small Unmanned Aircraft Systems cannot operate within this airspace without prior authorization.

Space that is not controlled:

Class F: Airspaces that are not controlled are known as airspace class F. Pilots operating within this airspace could be informed by Air Traffic Control but are not required to obtain approval and clearance.

Class G: It is another uncontrolled airspace , which spans the surfaces that border class E. Unmanned Aircraft vehicle operators do not require permission from Air Traffic Control to operate within the airspace.

OTHER CLASSIFICATIONS

Space for Special Use:

1. Prohibited Zones
2. Restricted Zones
3. Warn Zones
4. Military Operation Areas (MOAs)
5. Alert Regions
6. Controlled Firing Areas (CFAs)

Other AREAS:

1. Local Airport Advisory (LAA)
2. Military Training Route (MTR)
3. Temporary flight restriction (TFR)
4. Parachute Jump Aircraft Operations
5. Published VFR Routes
6. Terminal Radar Service Area (TRSA)
7. National Security Area (NSA)
8. Air Defence Identification Zones (ADIZ)
9. Aircraft Restricted Zones (FRZ) within the close vicinity of Capitol as well as White House

10. National Parks and request to operate at or above 2 000 AGL
11. National Oceanic and Atmospheric Administration (NOAA) Marine Areas off the coast that have the obligation to operate at or above the level of 2,000 AGL

Chapter 12: Aviation Weather Reporting

Understanding how weather functions is crucial for the successful flights around the globe. A Small Unmanned Aircraft vehicle operator should also pay attention to the weather reports in order to comprehend their significance for the Part107 test, and conduct efficient flight operations, regardless of whether for commercial or recreational purposes.

Reporting on Aviation Weather has been possible by the collaboration by the National Weather Service (NWS) and the

FAA (Federal Aviation Administration) and The Department of Defence (DOD) as well as other organizations that are that are involved in aviation.

Forecasts of weather aren't always 100% accurate, however they can help avoid accidents and crashes in the flight's operation.

WHAT IS THE WAY YOU CAN USE WEATHER OBSERVATION works:

The utilization of data is essential for the observation process. Data is collected from the upper and surface altitudes to calculate weather forecasts and forecasts.

SURFACE Aircraft OBSERVATION:

Surface Aviation observations use METAR (Meteorological Terminal Air Report) to gather weather-related elements on ground stations across in the United States. They are powered by the federal government and privately contracted with facilities that offer current information on climate conditions. METAR and other weather-related sources that are automated offer surface weather observations reports, as well as other pertinent information. METAR reports include station identification number, kind of report, date as well as the time, modifiables such as wind, visibility and more.

UPPER AIR OPERATION

Monitoring and forecasting upper air temperatures is more difficult. However, upper-air climate is possible to observe through PIREPs (Pilot reports). Upper air observations include clouds, humidity, turbulence size temperatures, temperature, icing pressure and wind information for altitudes of more than 100 feet. Flight pilots provide this information and are the sole source of information on high-altitude weather.

RADAR OBSERVATION:

Radar observations provide the following details: the weather, the winds, and weather systems. Radars such as WSR-88D NEXRAD WSR-88D NEXRAD offer sufficient information that informs people about the impending weather conditions. FAA terminal doppler radar (TDWR) that is located at the major airports helps in sending severe weather alerts as well as cautions to traffic officers at airports. They can also be extremely helpful in determining the weather conditions, and write reports.

Service outlets:

Service outlets are either government-owned or privately owned stations which meet the needs of aviation across the United States. Many different government agencies, like those of the Federal Aviation Administration (FAA), National Oceanic and Atmospheric Administration (NOAA) as well as the National Weather Service (NWS) are in partnership with private aviation companies to offer various ways for getting information about weather.

WEATHER BRIEFINGS

Before any flight departs pilots must be briefed about the specific weather conditions that pertain to the kind of flight. The briefings on weather are available from an expert in FSS, NWS, and AFSS.

Briefings on weather are comprised of three kinds: short briefings, standard briefings as well as an outlook briefing. These briefings are essential to the flight plan and can be utilized as a reference when the flight is lost.

STANDARD BRIEFING:

The typical briefing is a comprehensive report that contains information about the weather conditions that will affect the flight. It is compiled prior to the departure of the flight and is utilized in planning flights. A standard briefing will provide the following details:

ADVERSE CONDITIONS Adverse conditions are the information about conditions that can cause the cancellation or modification of an air flight. The conditions that are considered to be adverse and should be taken into consideration prior to taking off are the possibility of thunderstorms or icing.

VFR A flight is not recommended for: VFR refers to Visual Flight Rules. A flight could be cancelled or delayed if the weather conditions fall below the minimal rules established by the VFR. The pilot can decide which option to comply with the rules, however it is strongly recommended to take the information seriously.

Current conditions give information on the temperature, winds and visibility. If the flight takes more than two hours, the current conditions won't be mentioned during the presentation.

NOTAM (NOTICE to airmen) Note to airmen is an announcement or report published by the FAA which informs airmen and operators of aircrafts of any conditions or changes at an airport, and warns about any part or system of airspace which could impact the operation of the flight. For drones and sUAS, an airman's notice could be an interim restriction on flights due to any changes in any aspect of the airspace system.

Abbreviated Briefing It is a shortened version of the standard briefing. If a flight is delayed, information on the weather conditions that will be required to take off. usually required.

A OUTLOOK BRIEFING: An overview briefing is required in the event that a flight's departure is at least six hours away. It gives weather information that is only available due to the flight's timetable and may influence choices regarding the direction of flight , altitude and so on.

Chapter 13: Part Of 107 Practice Questions To Pass The Airman Skill Test

Questions for Part107 are based on weatherconditions, aircraft operations regulations, airspace requirements load, performance, and so on. An understanding of these subjects and sub-topics is beneficial when you are preparing for the airman test. In this regard Here are some questions you can practice in preparation to take the exam. The questions may include;

QUESTIONS:

1. It's 7:07 am. The official sunrise time is 7:40 am. The Unmanned Aircraft Vehicle does not include any lights for anti-collision. How long do you have to wait to fly in Part 107?

a. 10 minutes
b. 70 minutes
C. 40 minutes

2. When the centre of gravity on your plane is located too far forward (rearward) What is the likelihood of the outcome?

a. A. Aircraft is likely to have difficulty recovering from a stopped position

b. The aircraft won't be able to keep the same turn

C. It will be able to achieve higher airspeeds

3. An experienced wildlife photographer uses an sUAS mounted on an unmoving truck to take aerial photos of birds migrating in remote wetlands. The truck's drive is not a crew member's function in the operation. Does this sUAS operation in accordance to the 14 CFR Part 107?

A. In compliance with Part 107.

b. Not in compliance with Part 107

C. In violation of local and state traffic laws

4. You've agreed to tickets to football in exchange for the use of your sUAS for videotaping the construction zone of the future. What FAA rules will this sUAS operation is subject to?

a. 14. CFR Part 101

b. 14. CFR Part 107

. This operation isn't dependent on FAA regulations

5. To prevent a collision with an airplane that is not human-crewed you believe that your tiny aircraft with no crew reached an altitude of more than 600 feet above the ground. Who should you notify of the deviation?

a. A. National Transportation Safety Board

b. At the request of Federal Aviation Administration

C. Air Traffic Control

6. You're contemplating flying a drone in an area of about 4 miles to the north to Cochran Airport. According to the sectionsal map What is the height of the nearest obstacle that is in the vicinity?

a. 1568 feet Mean Sea Level

b. 1169 feet Mean Sea Level

c. 1568 feet Above Ground Level

7. You've been given a task to examine an area which is located within the Airspace Class C. Which of the following tasks must you complete prior to beginning the operation?

a. Prepare a risk mitigation plan and mitigation measures to the FAA

b. Contact the appropriate ATC (ATC) center.

C. The request for an airspace authorisation using LAANC and the FAA DroneZone

8. In accordance with Part 107 of the Part 107 rules, operations of drones from an automobile is permissible only when the following conditions are met:

a. It is carried out by a drone pilot licensed under Part 107.

b. It's carried out in a remote area

C. The Drone is visible to the eye

9. What is the minimum age required for an individual to be eligible to get Part 107 remote pilot certificate? Part 107 remote pilot certificate?

a. 16

b. 18

c. 21

10. In the course of commercial drone work If you're working for a drone company, your Drone has an accident and then crashes. Which of the following

scenarios do you not have to submit in the FAA?

a. Minor injury to someone that must be treated using first aid

b. Injuries that are serious and necessitates the patient to be hospitalized

C. The damage to a vehicle is estimated to cost $750 to fix

11. According to the current weather forecast the forecast predicts an altitude of 700 feet. In this regard how high is it possible to use your Drone?

a. 500 feet Above Ground Level

b. 400 feet Above Ground Level

c. 200 feet Above Ground Level

12. How often do drone pilots need to examine their Drone to make sure the drone is operating in good order?

a. Prior to every flight

b. Daily

C. Monthly

13. "Unmanned airplane" is described as a device that is that is operated.

a. In search and rescue activities that are not public

b. The aircraft is not subject to human intervention directly from inside or outside the plane

C. For recreational and hobby use only if it is not certified

14. Responsibility for collision avoidance within an alert zone lies in the hands of

a. The agency responsible for the control

b. All pilots

C. Air Traffic Control

15. Remote Pilots must finish the following operational area surveillance prior to sUAS flight:

a. Plan to keep participants at a safe the entire operation

b. Select an operational region which is populated

C. Maintain the operating area clear of obstructions and in a suitable distance from any non-participants

Conclusion

This book outlines the study plan. It provides the necessary weapons to deal with any questions you may be asked during the test. Part 107 of the airman knowledge test is presented in subtopics and topics that can be found here. A number of possible sample questions are also provided to the potential Unmanned Aircraft Pilot to prepare using.

But, it's not enough to take the test to memory without taking the time to study the numerous sections of information, topics, and other details that have been meticulously compiled throughout this publication. Make sure you are familiar with the different words, acronyms, terms and other terms related to aviation prior to deciding for the exam.

If you're thinking of making use of your small, unmanned aircraft for commercial use the book has offered a detailed outline of how to make the most of the business opportunities available and the limitations, registration process, and what you need you should consider prior to making a decision. Remote pilots who are recreational must think about the locations where they may operate their small aircrafts according to the rules set forth in this book.

Use this advice And you'll be well on your way to success.

Part 2

Introduction

Drones are a common sight these days. They are no longer a thing of the past that they were considered to be to be futuristic and only used in sci-fi films and utilized only by the largest militaries. Nowadays, they're all over the world, vloggers use them to make content. Media companies employ drones to report on events, film makers utilize drones to create films and even children have amusement with drones. In recent years, the growth of drones for civilian use has led to the huge growth in demand for drones, and sales are expected to exceed 7 million by 2020.

The explosive growth in use of drones is due to the revolutionary discoveries and advances within aerospace technologies, materials sciences as well as control and automation integrated circuits, and software development. These diverse fields have been integral in the development and design of drones for consumer use which we utilize every day.

The book we'll be taking an in-depth and detailed study of drones. We will look at the various components of drones and the way they function, as well as the various types and classifications that drones come in, the uses and the best way to maintain the drone.

Chapter 1: Is Titled Understanding

Drones

* What exactly are Drones?

Drones are a reference to the UAV (Unmanned aerial vehicles), RPAS (Remotely Piloted Aerial Systems) These are more appropriately defined by the term RC (remote control) devices that are remote controlled via the ground. The phrase "drone" was originally more of a term used by the military before it became popular for commercial use. Remote control systems that are that is used to control drones is similar to the ones employed for toys controlled by remotes that can be considered drones, since they are not manned also.

In recent years, drones have risen in popularity with a huge number of people. There are new models released each day, with improved and more advanced features. Some models are specifically designed for people who are just starting out and others come with memory cards and cameras that enable users to capture footage and transfer the footage to computers.

Controllers and transmitters are utilized to control a drone using making use of radio frequency. The more control channels have the better the quality.

* What can Drones be used To Do?

The majority of drones today are equipped with cameras which allows users to capture photos or videos whether for a career or as a leisure activity.

Have you ever witnessed drones in action or seen a video of drones? It is enough to convince you to buy to have one of your own. The possibilities using drones is constantly growing. Here are some of the things they are capable of:

Apart from flying for fun or creating the most stunning aerial photos and videos drones are also utilized for many other reasons.

Drone Racing:

The Drone Racing is an sport of competition which uses drones to race along a specified course. The races may take place either outdoors or indoors, and focus on avoiding obstacles that require the participant to be proficient in complex maneuvers. Most racing drones are designed to take into account speed, weight, and agility. speed.

Military:

Drones are employed by the military when the use of manned aircrafts is dangerous or in a way that is not appropriate. They were infamous because the US military employed them to conduct recon missions and for transporting arms-laden goods into enemy territory within Pakistan in Pakistan and Afghanistan throughout the Global War on Terrorism. Drones also serve as a means of crowd control using weapons like tear gas and sound cannons.

Constructions and Construction Sites Surveys:

This is among the most beneficial ways drones can be employed in the commercial field. Through the use of drones, individuals do not have to put their lives at risk in hazardous jobs like climbing up the walls to survey buildings.

High definition images from drones are of such high quality that they are able to be used to build 3D models.

Filmmaking and Journalism

Drone footage is a cost-effective method of capturing aerial shots for amateur and professional films. Aerial perspectives are also helpful for journalists to film situations like floods, warsand mass protests, etc.

Remote Sensing:

Drone photography is utilized by professionals to build 3D models of landscapes which aren't accessible via traditional methods. Utilizing technology like LiDAR (Light detection as well as Ranging) it creates an elevation model of the terrain as well as DEM (Digital Elevation Model) through the range of values generated by a drone's pulsed laser radar.

Making Deliveries:

The most well-known shipping companies such as DHL as well as Amazon have started to promote the drones used to deliver items. Delivery drones are equipped with claws that allow them to drop items gently from a distance away to the desired location. Drones can significantly accelerate the delivery of goods and also saving on operating and aerial expenses.

The Search and Rescue (SAR) drones could be used to speed up search and rescue in areas that aren't accessible due to natural disasters such as floods, earthquakes or floods. When humans working in search and rescue require rest and are exhausted after a time drones are not. There have been many successful stories of rescue missions completed with the help of drone footage.

For ecological and environmental reasons:

The high-definition pictures taken by drones can be used to assess the degree of erosion that occurs in coastal and hazardous zones. There is a constant development of drones equipped to collect water samples from rivers and lakes to make environmental oversight more efficient. Utilizing the thermal imaging capabilities of drones, drones can be used to observe the habitats of animals, in order to keep wildlife safe from poachers.

Atmospheric Science:

Drones are especially beneficial to collect aerial information about the atmosphere. Global Hawk, a drone Global Hawk that is utilized by NASA to study the impact of hurricanes and gather crucial information about the atmosphere via aerial photographs. Drones are also being utilized by researchers at Oklahoma to determine the level of the atmosphere in order to issue warnings about tornadoes for as much as an hour earlier than normal.

Chapter 2: Drone Controls

* What is the process by which Drones Function?

Drones are simple to fly, but equally difficult to fall over. They're not really as difficult to fly, though some people believe they are. The truth is that anyone who knows how to operate devices like smartphones and gaming consoles ought to be competent to fly drones. However, majority of drones require a basic understanding of the controls so that you don't be destroyed or crash into the ground. If you've a good knowledge of the way drones work and how they operate, you'll be able to fly a drone without fear.

To fully understand the way drones function first, you must be familiar with the basic elements of a drone.

Frame:

The frame is constructed using a number made of lightweight materials including fiberglass, carbon fiber etc. Light metalslike aluminum and titanium are often utilized. The frame serves as the central element of electronics within the drone.

Rotors are placed on spokes which diverge towards the outside beyond the hub on the majority of quadcopter frames.

The frame protects the motor, making it water-proof. Some models include guards for the rotor into the frame to protect the motor from damage and improve security for the user.

Motor:

The motor provides the rotors the power it requires to turn. To decrease friction and prolong the battery's life A lot of drones use brushless motors that improve efficiency and speed up flight times.

Battery:

A lithium polymer type of battery is used to supply energy to the rotors as well as other electronic components within the drone. These types of batteries are compact and light in weight. They also have large energy density, but also have a large discharge speed.

Propellers:

They are needed to allow the drone to move around, hover, turn and tilt. Variations in the speed of rotation of rotors aid in making the drone more precise and responsive maneuvers. The majority of drones come with propellers made of plastic and the ones that are more expensive are made from carbon fiber.

Camera:

The GoPro is among the most well-known brands to capture videos and photos using drones. They are small high-definition, compact, and offer a variety of settings.

Gimbal:

This feature is required to ensure image stabilization and three-dimensional rotation to mounted cameras. They also come with dampeners to neutralize vibrations during the taking of videos or photos to prevent problems. Without the gimbal, cameras will have no value.

GPS (Global Positioning System) Module:

GPS GPS is a satellite-based navigation system that makes use of an radio receiver to measure the height, location as well as the speed, time, and height that the drone is flying. It is the most accurate method of navigation. The more sophisticated the GPS system is, the more precise the information is. This lets the drone fly in safety and return the home base in case it lose radio contact or if the user instructs it to. It is also necessary for the GPS is also essential in order to set waypoints during autonomous flight.

ESC (Electronic Speed Controls):

Electronic speed controllers regulate how fast the motor runs, as well as the direction of the motor. They allow for better control of motor speed that are essential to ensure the drone's navigation.

Receiver:

It is an electronic radio that lets you manage drones via wireless. Signals are received from a radio receiver, which is linked to the control unit for the drone.

Flight Controller:

Flight controllers combine all the information from the receiver, GPS module ESC as well as the battery monitor and the other sensors onboard. This is the drone's brain in which all commands are issued to the controller to control the speed of the motor and rotor as well as trigger cameras. enable autopilot and failsafe precautions.

Things that could interfere with the Drone: After you've got an idea of the various components of a drone, you are aware that there are a variety of sensors in a drone but you should be aware that the surrounding environment could affect the sensors.

A sensor connects directly to one of these sensors is the GPS receiver. There are a variety of factors that could affect the GPS signal however the main reason is that you lose line-of-sight to satellites. This typically happens when you fly indoors in large forests mountains, in mountain ranges, or in cities that are tall.

Another sensor that could be affected can be affected is the compass. If this isn't present, the drone will not be able tell which direction it's facing and the GPS will not be able to navigate correctly. If the compass encounters interference, drones typically is flying in a circular pattern that gets more and more pronounced with time. It is important to land your drone and attempt to calibrate it when you notice it is flying in this way or else it could be destroyed.

Compass interference is among the main reasons for drone crashes because it's not something most people consider. Metal-based objects could affect the drone. This could refer to many objects in the world like parks benches or power lines that come from cars and metal structures, or even underground metal.

If you have an DJI drone it will alert you if it detects significant amounts of interference. It will ask whether you'd like to calibrate your drone's sensor. Be sure to not recalibrate your drone close to metal structures, or the calibration may be off. However, DJI drones feature dual redundancy of sensors This means they have a lower chance of experiencing interference than other drones.

The maximum range could be misleading. Based on the location you reside in the range could be greatly altered by interference from radios. If you fly close to radio towers, for example there is a chance that you will not have any range. The proximity of trees, mountains walls, walls, etc. could also impact the distance your drone is able to travel.

Another issue for long-distance drone operators is the height they need to fly to remain in their line-of-sight. The farther the drone is the lower the message it will receive. A majority of drones that have an integrated GPS will return home if they lose signal, however that doesn't mean it's going to return. If the drone encounters an error in its compass when it returns the drone may not be able to come back. It is therefore better to be cautious and to avoid losing signal.

Chapter 3: Drone Types

Types of Drones:

As drones have become increasingly well-known in recent years You've probably seen them advertised all over the place. If you've decided to join in the fun and buy drone, it's the most straightforward decision to make about the procedure. Because when you talk about the word "drone" isn't only mean one type there are many varieties that come with different characteristics.

What kinds of drones do we have?

The types of drones range from basic to expensive, and include photography racing, etc. Each drone model comes with distinct characteristics strengths, weaknesses, and strengths.

The most well-known drones are quadcopters. They typically have the shape of an H or X and is powered by four rotors and two sets of propellers that turn clockwise and counter-clockwise. A gyroscope or accelerometer determines the position of the drone within the sky.

Based on this data the rotors' position can be adjusted in order for drones to hover in one spot.

Quadcopters are also renowned for their safety and mobility and are often used by beginner users. You could, for example protect the rotors by putting them in propeller guards in order to minimize the risk of damage.

Beginner Drones:

They have a limited distance and a short time to fly However, they are economical and simple to fly. They are lightweight, compact which makes them safe and suitable for flying indoors. Their equipment and size makes them hard to operate outdoors, particularly in windy conditions. Models with cameras can capture poor quality videos and photos. Toy drones can be useful to get a feel for flying before you purchase the more expensive models or for people who desire to fly a drone to have enjoyment.

Hobby Drones:

They're also tough and inexpensive, however, they come with more sophisticated features than drones for beginners and usually require more experience to use. They offer a wider range of features and may include cameras with specialized features or other features that allow them to be used for recreational usage without not being anything more than basic.

Photography Drones:

These drones are specifically designed to fly in the open air and are ideal to take aerial photos. They tend to be heavier, larger and cost more than the other two drones. To ensure you are getting the most value with these drones, it's essential that they have the gimbal, or fixed camera. The other important feature it should include the quality of the camera, the megapixels, video resolution, automatic flight modes and obstacles to avoidance.

Racing Drones:

They are small quadcopters designed for speed as well as speed and endurance. They're typically used to participate at FPV(First-Person View) racing and other drone-related events. They can be capable of speeds up to 100 mph when diving. The components can be changed to increase the drone's acceleration, speed, and control. Fixed cameras aid the user in maneuvering the drone like they were inside it high-performance controllers alter the motor's power , allowing the drone to accelerate and slow it down quickly as they can.

Chapter 4: Flying Your Drone

* Beginner's Advice:

Be sure to keep your track of your flight time. Because they run on batteries, drones can only have the ability to fly for a short period of time. Certain drones will inform you when they are in the middle of its battery charge However, it is recommended to maintain your own timer so that you do not get lost in the shuffle.

Go through the manual thoroughly to ensure you understand the drone's operation and the features it comes with.

Every drone owner needs an extra battery. Due to how short the time a drone can fly it isn't a good idea to get stuck in the middle of things every now and then to recharge your battery.

It's recommended to lower the settings of your drone to make it more sluggish and more comfortable to fly the first time. Adjust them as you gain experience in flying.

Allow the drone to remain in the air for a short period of time after it has been on the ground. This allows the drone's systems some time to become familiar with the surroundings first. It also allows you to determine whether the drone is stable and is ready to fly.

Use only the emergency land feature only in emergency situations because it can complete shut down the motor which causes the drone to drop to the ground. This could cause damage to the drone or hurt any person in the vicinity.

Be aware of the indicators lights. They're not meant to be cool, but they serve a function. The indicators indicate to the operator the direction they should be facing. For instance: your drone may be sporting blue lights in the front, and red lights in the back. If you can see the blue lights pointing towards you it's an indication to turn your drone to allow it to return to you. These drones are especially useful in the dark, which means it is possible to fly your drone when you're not in the vicinity of any lights.

Do not focus on the additional features. A majority of drones can be capable of doing incredible things, such as taking off at long altitudes, and performing tricks but as a novice do not attempt to perform these feats at this point. Learn the basics of flying. Once you're comfortable with them, you can begin to look into all the other options.

Check for safe areas for drones within your local area prior to deciding to fly to ensure that you don't get into difficulties later.

Always ensure that the drone is in your view. relying on the First-Person-View of the drone could result in injuries since you will not be able to recognize obstacles at the right time.

Don't think that you can get a lot from drones priced under $500. You won't have the awesome features like the ability to avoid obstacles and video of high quality If you don't plan to shell out for it.

If you are in the US you must declare your drone as a commercial device if its weight is greater than 0.55 pounds, and under 55 pounds. It is necessary to be 13 years old in order to register.

Always remove the drone's battery when you're doing work on one, since the drone may suddenly turn on.

To stop that the drone is wobbling, and an uncomfortable flight, ensure your propellers remain in a balanced position.

You should consider purchasing prop guards to protect the drone. Also, consider purchasing additional propellers that are always ready in the event that a propeller breaks.

You could consider the use of drone simulators in order to keep practicing in adverse conditions.

Avoid flying near to animals. The sound waves released by drones causes anxiety for the birds and could cause them to hit your drone. Switch off the VPS in the event that you believe your drone could hurt a bird or reverse.

Avoid flying in reverse, particularly when you're not within sight of the drone, or else you could crash into an unnoticed obstruction.

Consider investing in an LCD monitor to can always see exactly what's on the other side of your drone. It can also aid you in capturing the most beautiful photos with no needing to imagine what the image will appear.

Try flying without the GPS to prepare for a GPS malfunctions or software malfunctions that could result in you losing control of your drone.

You should think about purchasing an GPS tracker in the event that it happens that the drone's GPS system malfunctions and it isn't able to find its way home , or if it gets lost.

Do you really trust yourself to not harm the expensive model of your drone? Learn from a certified expert you to fly the drone. DJI offers a no-cost workshop targeted at beginners to help you learn everything you should learn about flying drones. If you're not in the vicinity of the nearest DJI store, you can search for a similar event in your local area.

Fly confidently. Even if you've never had the privilege of flying a drone before don't let fear ruin your experience.

* Tips to Take Care of the Battery in your Drone:

Always ensure that you have a fully charged battery prior to boarding a plane in order to prevent getting into a mess.

Be sure your battery has been properly connected on the drone. Before you begin flying, switch off the remote control, then insert your battery in the drone. then press the Power Button on the battery and press and hold it again to switch off the drone. Do not remove a powered-on battery.

Be aware of the temperature in the surrounding environment. Make sure to only use the battery in temperatures between -10 degree Celsius and 40 degrees Celsius to ensure safety. If temperatures are low, let the drone hover for about one minute to heat up the battery. The battery will warm up automatically. If temperatures are higher than 40 degrees Celsius pay attention on the temp of your battery. If it's more than 65 degrees Celsius reduce the drone's altitude. Anything higher than 65 degrees could trigger the battery's on fire and possibly explode.

Before you remove the battery following the flight, shut off the drone in first. Switch off the controller at the end.

Keep the battery in a dry, cool location at temperatures ranging from 22 and 28 degrees Celsius. Do not place the battery in sunlight or near fires, stoves or other sources and keep it clear of liquids. Don't also store the battery in items with metal components, like watches, glasses or other such items.

If you don't intend to be using the battery for longer than 10 consecutive days charge it up to 40-65% power prior to the storage. When the battery has been fully charged while stored, it could get older faster. In the event that the battery was kept at a lower than 10% capacity, it may be discharged too high.

Before transferring a battery, ensure that it has been fully charged, which is around 50% power (5 percent when you board an airplane). Place the battery in a transport box prior to the transportation. During transport, be sure that the battery doesn't be damaged by external forces, like falling, hitting other objects, etc.

Make sure to use a certified charger, or your battery could be damaged. Avoid charging the battery when it's hot, for example immediately after a flight or your battery's life could reduce.

* Drone-related Acronyms:

First Person View - FPV

FPS is Frames Per Second.

GHz - Gigahertz

FAA - Federal Aviation Agency

GPS - Global Positioning System

RC Remote Control Remote Control

LCD - Liquid Crystal Display

* Restrictions and Rules on Drones: Drones:

If you are a drone owner for the first time it is important to know the rules in your nation when it comes to drones flying. Here are a few of the best rules that are applicable to all nations:

Do not fly higher than 400 feet above the ground.

Do not fly in the vicinity of airports.

Do not fly too close to other people.

Do not fly over areas that are prone to disasters like floods or fires.

Avoid the scene of crime. Let the police get on with their work.

Avoid flying over government buildings such as national parks or private property.

"Join an Drone Community:

Each drone owner must be a part of at minimum one community, regardless of whether it's online or offline. There are numerous online forums that are specifically for drone owners on the Internet that cover virtually every subject you could require an answer to. Who better to seek assistance than other drone owners who have similar drones like they...

Chapter 5: Drones Buying Guide -

Features

If you buy drones, it doesn't mean that you'll be able to remove it from the packaging and anticipate it to start flying in a matter of minutes. Make use of the following abbreviations to see what you receive.

BNF: Bind-N-Fly

The product includes everything, except for the controller. For these kinds of models, you need choose between an existing controller or, if compatible or locate the controller separately and connect that controller to the receiver included in the package. It is important to note that there isn't a assurance that a controller and receiver will work even if they operate on identical frequencies. It could have been that way in analog communications however, with the advent of digital communications it is also possible to use the same manufacturer protocol. Before you purchase the drone, make sure you check whether your controller is compatible with the drone.

ARF: Nearly ready to fly

The item must be assembled before it can fly. The drone kits typically do not include the receiver or controller, and could also include other parts like batteries, motors, ESCs, etc. If you come across ARF as the name, be sure you review the product's description first. ARF models are great for those who enjoy working in DIY project.

RTF Ready to Fly

The product is all in one piece and contains everything required to get flying within a couple of minutes after being removed from the box. The majority of the time, you only need to perform basic tasks like charging the battery, attach the drone's controller, and attach the propellers.

• Drones:

If you're looking to buy a drone your first purchase, you could be overwhelmed by the options. There is of course an expense to show the quality of the drone, but to get more educated it is essential to be aware of the specifications. Here are a few most beneficial characteristics:

Battery Life: A time of flight could vary between 5 and 30 minutes, based on different factors like the model of drone, battery, and the dimensions. The majority of beginner drones run for 5-10 minutes. It could be the end of your flight, or simply replace the battery. Some drone owners carry additional batteries in their bags so that they are always prepared to replace them should they need to continue flying the drone.

If you don't want the extra features offered by the more expensive drones, replacing batteries is a cheaper alternative to buying one that has an extended flight time. Don't be fooled into thinking that you don't require an additional battery. The fact is that no matter which model you own you never know what you could find yourself in an event where it would have been beneficial and spare your trip to the store to recharge your battery before.

Headless Mode A drone has an front and back side. It means that when you and your drone are facing in each other in the same direction then using the directional stick will cause it to fly left when you press left. If the drone is turned in the opposite direction and is facing your direction, the directions will be reversed. This can be extremely confusing for newbies and is often the primary cause of crashes.

The headless mode can solve this issue. It is activated that allows the drone to fly in identically to the direction of the remote. This means that it must always be in the direction that you intended. It's definitely a useful option for in case you need to fly the drone without having to constantly check its direction. Don't become accustomed with this option if plan to fly higher-quality as well as more expensive drones later on in the near future.

Brushless Motors: These type of motors are priced higher than brush motors. They have longer life and provides a quieter performance.

Return Home function This function does exactly what it claims to do. When you press an button, it brings the drone back to its original place. This is an extremely useful option for those times those times when you lose control of your drone or simply wish to bring it back to a safe location.

But, this feature isn't the same for every model.

If you are using this feature on a drone powered by GPS it is recommended to be patient and wait for the drone's position via the GPS satellite prior to pressing"Return Home Home.

When making use of this option on a less expensive model that does not have the GPS feature, the drone just allows the drone to fly forward. To ensure that it doesn't fail it is best to use return Home button only when you are in the Headless mode. If you do not, your drone could take off in the reverse direction instead of the location it's required.

Following-me mode: Drones equipped with GPS functions provide this feature. The mode lets the drone follow you and track your movements on the ground or water, allowing you to concentrate on what you're doing as the drone keeps track of your movements. Certain drones work better with this feature than others If this is a feature that you would like to have, be sure to select one suitable for the task.

Obstacle Avoidance The feature is a premium feature that is available on some of the most expensive drones. It can cost lots of money, however, it will shield your drone from hitting objects like trees. Similar to the follow-me mode certain drones are more effective than others. Check out what other people have said about it to ensure that it functions as intended.

Camera: This is a common feature for most drones. If you are looking for the best possible quality footage, then you should take the camera specs into consideration. Cheap drones usually include a camera as an add-on part, giving you a choice to install it or not. If you don't plan to take photos or record videos, then it is recommended not to put it on the drone because the extra weight and stress on the drone will drain its battery faster and reduce its flight time. If you want to attach the camera, however, you should note that some drones rely on their own add-on cameras, while others can attach action cameras such as a GoPro.

Many of the camera features can be changed to your liking, including the shutter speed, and the size of the photo or video, etc.

Range: Every drone has a limited range on how far it can be controlled. For beginner quadcopters, the range can vary from 50 to 100 meters. For more advanced drones, the range can go up to as much as 5000 meters. So, depending on what you want to use the drone for, you should keep this in mind.

Gimbal: This is a device that helps maintain a stable camera footage, no matter which direction the drone tilt. The gimbal works by keeping the camera leveled by providing pivoted support. It is a very important feature for those that aim to take a lot of videos.

Chapter 6: Buying Guide –

Recommendations

and Prices

● Five Factors To Consider Before Buying a Drone:
Flight Time: Most drones have a somewhat poor flight time, but differ from model to model. To show just how far apart it can be: A cheap model like the Syma X5C, for instance, has an average time of about 7 minutes, while a more expensive model like the DJI Phantom 2 Vision Plus averages around 15 to 20 minutes.
Skill Level: If you buy a drone that is beyond your skill level, you will most probably end up crashing it sooner than later and waste your money. Drones such as the Blade Nano QX include SAFE technology which helps to stabilize it. So keep this in mind if you don't have much confidence in your skills.

Camera Specs: Cameras differ depending on the type of drone you pick. Cheaper models, for instance, don't include FPV capabilities and have poor resolution. But if you are not aiming to be a professional, then even a low-quality camera is better than nothing.

GPS Sensors: These sensors offer quite a lot of useful features on its own. You can set coordinates and let the drone fly there automatically, and even let the drone find its way back home when you recall it. Keep this in mind if you plan to fly the drone at long distances.

Controllers: You won't be able to control your drone without this. Generally, the controllers consist of two analog sticks and have a 2.4GHz frequency. Some controllers can show real-time diagnostics such as throttle position, height, speed, etc, while others like the Hubsan X4 H107D even include built-in LCD monitors on their controllers.

Let's look at some examples of the best, but cheapest, drones in each category:

- Beginner Drones:

Here are 3 of the cheapest, but reliable, drones you can start practicing with. These are able to take a few hits and have easy accessible spare parts to buy if you should have to replace something.

Syma X5HC:

Estimated Price 65.99$

This drone is one the latest beginner drones and is very light, but sturdy. It has a flying time of about 7 to 9 minutes, a flight distance of about 30 to 50 meters, and includes a 2MP detachable camera that is capable of taking very nice, clear shots for a drone this cheap. Hover mode is a new addition to the Syma X5 range and enables the drone to hover in the air above a certain altitude even if the user lets go of the controller.

Ryze Tello:

Estimated Price - $99.00

This drone exists thanks to the collaboration between DJI, Ryze, and Intel. These companies created the drone together for kids to have an educational, engaging, and fun experience with drones. The flight time of the drone is about 13 minutes with a maximum flight distance of about 100 meters.

The Tello drone consists of a 5MP/720p camera which is capable of taking pictures and videos of rather good quality. Even though the unit doesn't include a gimbal, the video is steady enough to expect smooth shots.

On its bottom, you can find VPS (vision positioning sensors), which allow drones to hover in place and keep stable in both indoors and outdoors experiences.

It also has a built-in EZ shots feature that allows the drone to record shots automatically.

Another interesting feature is the different flight modes, including the 8D Flips which can flip the drone in 8 different directions when you swipe the screen. The drone will remain stable after each flip because of the VPS.

HolyStone F181:

Estimated Price - $99.99

This quadcopter is pretty impressive for a beginner, mainly because of its 2 unique features. There are 4 rotation speeds that vary from 40, 60, 80, and 100 mph, which helps you to start slow and gradually improve your flying experience. The next unique feature is its Headless Security System, which ensures that the drone doesn't get lost. It has a flight time of 7 to 9 minutes, a flight range of 50 to 100m, a maximum speed of 10mph, and a 2MP camera.

- Camera Drones:

These type of drones are the most popular, mostly because drones keep getting smarter and easier to use with every produced model. They consist of features such as avoiding obstacles, keeping the focus on a specific target while flying, being able to follow pre-selected paths, etc.

DJI Spark

Estimated Price - $569.00

This is a small, portable drone from DJI, which can easily fit on the palm of your hand. But even though it's small, it's packed with features. It includes a 12MP Full HD 1080P camera that shoots at 30 frames per second, a 2-axis gimbal for camera stabilization, 16 minute max flight time, 31 mph max speed, and is very intelligent. The DJI Spark only need hand gestures to control its movements, which makes it the best option for taking selfies. Just raise your palm in the air and the drone will follow, wave to it and it will move away, motion it to come back to have it fly toward you again. The drone is so advanced that it doesn't require you to do much for it to take great shots.

Yuneec Q500+ Typhoon

Estimated Price - $599.00

Yuneec produces exceptional high-quality drones and is considered to be one of DJI's greatest rivals. If you are looking for a semi-professional drone that includes a camera, then this is a great choice. The camera is a CGO2+ with a 16MP sensor and is capable of taking FULL HD videos at 60fps. The flight time is about 25 minutes and even includes 2 batteries with the order. The controller is an ST-10+ Ground Station which is a great advantage to flying because of its built-in 5.5" Android touchscreen.

DJI Mavic Air:
Estimated Price - $999.00
This drone is a recent release from DJI and is extremely portable, making it the perfect choice for people who travel often, vloggers, and basically anyone on the go. It also includes features that most people would want in a drone, such as a 4K camera that is capable of shooting slow motion shots at 120fps/1080P, a 3 direction obstacle avoidance, a dual satellite system which assists with safety and precision flying, autonomous flight modes, etc. It has a flight time of around 21 minutes, 3 different speed modes, a 6.2-mile flight distance, and includes 2 extra batteries with the order.

- FPV Racing Drones:

These drones are built for one purpose and that is to compete in FPV races. They are different from both beginner and photo/video drones, because they usually trade flight time and convenience for performance and speed. With speeds of up to 100mph, they are highly mobile and a real pain to control.

Racing drones are only meant for people with experience, not beginners. If someone without experience should attempt to fly one, it could lead to serious damage to a person, animal, vehicle, or property due to high speeds.

Many people who fly FPV racing drones build their own. It is useful too, because if something should break, then they would know exactly how to repair it. It is also less expensive to gather and build the parts yourself rather than buying the RTF version.

The parts necessary to build such a drone include:
-Frame
-4 motors
-4 propellers
-4 ESCs
-Antennas
-FPV Body Camera
-FPV monitor or goggles
-Video transmitter and receiver
-Radio transmitter and receiver
-Remote Controller
-Battery straps

But if you do not have the patience to build one or are just interested in the fun of flying one without the struggle, then you should look at the list below:

ARRIS X-Speed 250B RTF
Estimated Price - $309.00
This drone has a carbon/glass fiber body which is high quality for its price. It includes everything, except a battery, for you to get it airborne. The recommended battery for this product is a Lipo 3S or 4S.

The flying time is around 10 minutes, has brushless motors, high efficiency 3 blade propellers, a 700TVL HD camera, etc. The camera is divided from the main frame by vibration dampening balls with a slider on the top plate for you to adjust the FPV camera tilt angle.

Lumenier QAV210-RTF Charpu Edition
Estimated Price - $398.39
This drone has a carbon fiber frame which helps to make it extra durable. The 210 in its name is related to its 210mm size. It comes already set up, tested, and pretty much ready to fly, but you have to buy your own radio receiver. It has a built-in 1080P HD camera, but also supports HD cameras like the GoPro.

EACHINE Wizard X220S
Estimated Price - $459.99
This quadcopter is one of the most popular for FPV racing, mostly because of its wide availability and low price. It is equipped with 2300kv Motors, an SP Racing F3 Flight Controller, BL Heli 20Amp

ESCs, a basic FPV System, a 700TVL FPV Camera, 200mw 5.8ghz Video Transmitter, a 1500mAH Lipo battery, and comes with enough spare propellers so that you have the freedom to fly it to your heart's content. You will have to set up your own receiver and tweak the flight controller with Betaflight, but once you have it all set up, the drone will reward you with powerful, adrenaline-filled performance.

Chapter 7: Buying Guide – Insurance

- Where To Buy A Drone

The Top 5 Websites People Usually Buy Drones From:

dji.com: DJI is both number 1 in popularity and name. If you want to buy a DJI drone, it is recommended to buy directly from DJI since they update their drones with small changes every few weeks. These changes are usually aimed to improve reliability and safety and might be hardware or software related. So if you buy it from retailers, you might not get the latest version of the drone. Another reason is the DJI's accidental damage protection program you get at checkout, which will help you should you crash your drone while learning the basics on the first day. DJI also offers free shipping, so you have no reason not to order from them.

Amazon.com: They are one of the most popular online shops with a large variety of drones and parts for everyone's' needs.

getfpv.com: They offer high-quality FPV components, frames, etc.

HobbyKing.com: For hobby enthusiasts, this is one of the biggest stores. They often have thousands of products on sale that are either produced by themselves or the same as any other retailer. But like most places, Hobby King comes with its ups and downs, so you should read the reviews in order to determine which products are good or not.

HeliPal.com: They are established in Hong Kong and have products from popular brands such as DJI, Tarot, Walkera, etc.

- Drone Insurance:

Drone insurance is not a requirement, but that doesn't mean you should not get it. It is important not just because it will save you money if your drone gets damaged or stolen, but will also protect you financially in situations where your drone injures someone or damage someone's property.

Who should buy Drone Insurance?
If you only have a basic beginner or hobby drone, then insurance coverage is a bit extreme and expensive.
But if you are a serious drone operator and do something like professional photography, then you should seriously consider getting insurance.
The type of insurance depends on the drone's cost, where you usually fly it, and what it is used for.

Drone insurance types are always changing, but here are some of the basic types to consider.

Liability Insurance
Liability insurance is the most common, but also the most important type of drone insurance and is recommended to get

before considering other types of insurance.

It protects you financially from any third party claims that include injury to a person or damage to property. For example, if you were to unexpectedly lose control of the drone and let it fly into a crowd, a car, or a building, you could be held liable for huge sums of medical costs, repair costs, etc. The insurance will then take over the responsibility of paying for the claims.

- Hull Insurance

Hull insurance covers any accidental damage that might occur to your drone. For example, if you lose control of the drone and it hits the wall, the insurance will either pay for the repair or for a full replacement.

Note that some insurers don't cover the onboard equipment, so if the camera is damaged from a fall, the hull insurance might not pay for it.

Payload Insurance

You need the Payload insurance if you want to cover all those expensive equipment on your drone. Usually the attachments are more likely to be damaged than the drone itself. Just a small, insignificant fall from a chair or a table can break or damage the camera or sensors. The insurance will pay for any accidental damage or for a full replacement.

Chapter 8: Flying Your Drone -

Getting Started

- Beginner - How to fly a Quadcopter:

Where to Begin?
When you buy a drone, there usually isn't much information to teach you how to fly one. So you might be tempted just to pick up the controller and start flying around without having a clue what you are doing. But it is important to note that quadcopters are very powerful with rapid rotating propellers that can break or damage the things it crashes into very easily, or even break the expensive drone itself.

How to Use the Controls:
If you are used to playing video games, you've most probably used a twin-stick controller before, so the basic setup of a

Radio Transmitter will immediately feel familiar.

The controller consists of two main sticks which control the throttle and direction with switches which are optional and often used for switching flying modes, turning LEDs on or off, etc.

Usually on the left stick, you will find:

1. Throttle: Use the up and down axis to make the quadcopter ascend or descend at varying speeds.

2. Yaw: Use the left and right axis to rotate the quadcopter clockwise or counter-clockwise.

Usually on the right stick, you will find:

3. Pitch: Use the up and down axis to tilt the quadcopter forward or backward.

4. Roll: Use the left and right axis to tilt the quadcopter left or right.

Trim: Buttons that adjust the throttle, yaw, pitch, and roll if they are off balance.

These controls are also known by other names:

- Yaw - rudder

- Pitch - elevator
- Roll - aileron

Maneuvering Definitions:

1. Hover - To stay in the same position while in the air. Do this by controlling the throttle.

2. Bank turn - To make a steady circular motion in either clockwise or counterclockwise position.

3. Figure 8 - To fly in a figure 8 shape.

There are Normally 3 Types of Flight Modes:

1. Manual, also known as rate, hard, or Acro.

This is like flying a helicopter. If you roll the quadcopter it will not return to its original position. Even if the quadcopter returns to the middle when you let go of the stick, it will still stay tilted.

2. Attitude, also known as self-level or Auto-level.

The quadcopter levels itself out when the sticks are centered.

3. GPS-hold, also known as Loiter.

This is almost the same as auto-level, but it uses a GPS. When the sticks have been centered, the quadcopter returns to its position.

Before You Start Flying Your Drone:
Things to keep in mind to have the best flying experience:
•   Fly in the morning to have a reduced chance of there being wind.
•   Fly in a big, open area like a park or grass field.
•   Don't fly near people and animals.
•   Always stay focused. Don't get distracted.
•   Never do something you know you are not capable of.

● Tips for Flying Drones:

1. Choose a Safe Spot to Practice Flying Your Drone:
For beginners, it's better to practice in conditions that favor you to decrease the possibility of crashing the drone. These conditions refer to big, open environments

free from any obstacles. Don't practice near areas with tall structures, electric cables, trees, and bodies of water or you might not be able to retrieve your drone if you should crash it. Fly during days when there are no wind and the weather is clear.

2. Practice Basic Moves First:

The first thing you must learn when practicing flying your drone, is how to hover. You should practice hovering at low altitudes of around 5 feet at first and then gradually increase the height when you feel comfortable with it. To land smoothly is another skill you should learn early to prevent damaging your drone.

When you have mastered the above, you can start with the basic moves such as moving in the direction you want it to and rotating. If your drone doesn't have headless mode, you will have to get used to navigating it as it won't always face the same direction as you. After this, you can move on to more difficult moves like flying in a square and circle pattern, or a figure of eight. With regular practice, you will be able to do even more advanced maneuvers.

3. Know the Flight Laws:

Depending on your location, it might be required for you to know the local laws of drone flights before you start practicing. The FFA, for example, requires you to register your drone if it weighs more than 0.55 pounds. The laws might also limit the maximum height you can fly your drone, or that you can only fly drones during the day. Some locations, such as airports or heavily populated areas, are naturally off-limits for flying drones. So, do your research beforehand to prevent being penalized or even have your drone confiscated.

4. Safety Tips:

Quadcopters are dangerous if you are not careful with them. Keep these precautions in mind to be safe:

- Don't touch the propellers while they are spinning, or you might just lose a few fingers!
- If you learn to fly indoors, it is best to tie the quadcopter down or surround it with something to prevent accidents.
- Always do a preflight and calibration check before you fly.

Chapter 9: Flying Your Drone - Basic Maneuvers

- Basic Steps on How to Start Flying a Quadcopter:

How to Get the Drone Off the Ground and into the Air:
Now that you have some understanding about the controls and necessary safety measures, you can start to fly your drone.

- You only need to use the throttle to lift the drone into the air.
- Push the throttle axis up slowly so that the propellers start to spin, then stop.
- Repeat this process a few times until you are comfortable with the sensitivity of the throttle.
- Once you are comfortable, gradually push the throttle until the drone starts lifting from the ground. Then push the throttle back so that the drone returns to the ground.

• Repeat this about 5 times while you check if the drone is steady.

• If it does move in any way other than up or down without you pressing the axis, then use the necessary trim button in order to balance these movements. For instance, if the drone moves to the left when you use the throttle, then adjust the "roll" trim button which is located next to the right stick.

• Repeat this trimming process until the drone is more stable while getting airborne.

How to Hover and Land Your Drone:

Now that you know how to get your drone off the ground, the next thing you should learn is how to hover in mid-air.

• Use throttle to get the drone about a foot into the air.

• Use the right stick to make small adjustments in order to keep the drone in hover position. You might also have to use the left stick to keep the drone from turning if needed.

• Bring the throttle back to zero slowly until the drone is an inch from the ground, then cut the throttle completely so that the drone drops to the ground.

• Repeat the process until you are confident to hover the drone in mid-air and to land it as gently as possible.

How to Move Your Drone Forward, Backward, Left, and Right:

In order to move the drone in any direction, you have to hold the throttle at a constant speed so that it remains airborne. Then use the right stick to move the drone in the desired direction.

• Let your drone hover in the air.

• To make it go forward, gently push the right stick forward.

• Pull the stick back to its original point.

• Now repeat this process with the backward, left, and right direction. If the drone starts to rotate, adjust the left stick to keep it in position.

• Sometimes when you move the drone in any direction, it might drop altitude. Just push the throttle so that it receives more power when you move or turn the drone and it should stay at the same altitude.

How to Rotate Your Drone:

•   Use the throttle to get your drone in the air.

•   While hovering, push the left stick either left or right and the drone will rotate in place.

•   Rotate the drone 360 degrees and then switch directions to rotate it 360 degrees in the opposite direction.

•   That's it. Keep doing it until you are comfortable.

How to Fly in Patterns:

Now that you know how to fly your drone in the four basic directions, it is time to use those skills to start flying in patterns. Always let the drone face away from you the whole time while flying in a pattern.

Square pattern:

- Fly forward a couple of feet and then hover in place for a few seconds.
- Now fly to the right the same amount of feet and hover in place.
- Fly backward next and hover.
- Lastly, fly left to return the drone to its original position.
- You have just made a successful square. Do this until you are confident before moving to the next pattern.

Circle pattern:
You must use the throttle, pitch, and roll at the same time in order to fly in a circle pattern.
- Get the drone airborne by using the throttle and decide if you are going to fly clockwise or counterclockwise. Let's assume you chose clockwise:
- Start by pushing the right stick diagonally up and to the right. This will simultaneously activate both the pitch and roll and start moving the drone in a circle to the ride side.

• Wait a few seconds, then rotate the right stick a bit more to the right to roll the drone more to the right.

• After a few more seconds, bring the right stick diagonally to the bottom and to the right. Carry on circling the right stick until the drone returns to its original location.

• You have just made a successful circle. Try and do it counterclockwise next by rotating the stick in the other direction. If the drone starts to rotate or face a different direction, adjust the drone's jaw.

How to Fly Your Drone Continuously:
To fly a drone continuously, you will have to get used to rotating and changing directions at the same time. What makes it difficult is that the drone will be facing different angles which require you to stay focused on how the movement sticks affect the drone's flight.

• Start by getting your drone in the air and let it hover.

• Rotate the drone to a small angle.

- Move the drone with the right stick to make it fly forward, backward, left, and right.
- Now rotate the drone to another angle and move it again so that you can get used to flying it while facing different directions.
- Repeat the process until you are comfortable to fly your drone at different angles.
- Now, push the right stick forward while simultaneously pushing the right stick a bit to the left/right.
- While doing the above, use yaw on the left stick to change the drone's direction.
- Adjust the drone's height by moving the throttle on the left stick up or down.

And that is all there is to it. Practice until you have complete control over your drone's movements.

Beginner Techniques to Master:
- Hovering a drone,
- Rotate the drone to different angels.

- Fly the drone in different directions while it is facing you.
- Fly at different altitudes.
- Fly the drone in a square pattern.
- Fly the drone in a circle pattern.
- Choose two targets on the ground and then fly and land on each one a few times.

Chapter 10: Advanced - Flying A Drone Like A Pro

Manual Flight Mode:
This mode lets you fly fast and do advanced moves without the drone's alignment and stabilization features. It might sound like fun but be sure to get the hang of the basics first in automatic mode. Once you are comfortable flying with all the features your drone offers turned on, especially in windy weather, then you can give the manual mode a try.

Have Some Fun with Your Drone:
Once you have the hang of the basics, you can start practicing some interesting moves. There are a lot of stunts to try if your drone supports it, such as a 360 degree forward, backward, or side flip, flying through an obstacle race alone or with a friend, practicing precise flying, etc. Find the Right Way to Hang:

The ability to hover is among of the most essential skills you can master. It doesn't matter if are about to take off, need to be able to control the drone, or you simply desire to land with ease like a pro It is essential to know how to get your drone to an immediate hover. Being able hover will allow you to capture the most stable, high-quality photos and videos. Begin by practicing near the ground at beginning and then move to the sky once you're at ease. Start by practicing hovering when the drone is moving at a slow speed, and then moving fast. Be aware of how the winds, the wind's momentum and speed influence the drone's behavior and soon you'll be capable of hovering in almost every circumstance.

The dangers of flying through Windy Conditions:

A drone can be difficult to control in windy conditions. This is why you must make sure the weather is calm when you're still experimenting. It will allow you to experience how the drone performs in clear weather , which will help you manage it if the wind picks up abruptly. If you observe that the wind speeds up in speed and reaches the speed of 10 miles an hour then you must place your drone in the air or you risk losing control and causing the risk of causing damage. You may think you're in control but it's not worth defying nature in order to make a fact. It's impossible to predict what happens when an unexpected, strong blow of wind takes your drone away.

What should you do if your Drone is Not Working?

It happens to everyone eventually, and if are skilled enough, you can make landing more comfortable and minimize harm. If you are certain that the drone is bound to crash, take care to keep the drone from obstacles first. Prior to the drone hitting the ground, instantly turn the throttle until it is at a level that the blades cease spinning as soon as it hits the ground. This is so that it minimizes damage to the motor as well as the blades and also harm to the object that you crash into.

* Steps to Advanced on Flying with a Quadcopter:

How to Fly with an 8-Pattern

This is similar as learning to fly using circles and squares however, it is more difficult.

To start flying with an 8-pattern

* Get your drone airborne.

Follow the same steps to make circles.

* Fly the drone in a clockwise circular.

When the circle is completed and you are ready to change direction, instantly switch into an anticlockwise circle, in a mirror-like manner.

The easiest method to master this pattern is to use two objects, like cones, between them, in the form of an eight.

Begin by making an enormous figure 8 pattern and then increase the difficulty by creating a smaller figure-8 pattern.

How to make Bank Turns:

It is by far the fastest, smoothest method of turning quadcopters.

To do a bank turn:

* This technique requires that you first create some forward speed first. This means that you need to move the pitch

control forward and then adjust the throttle so that it remains at a level the height.

* For a quadcopter with six axes to turn, you'll have to maintain forward pitch, while simultaneously applying the roll as well as yaw controls in the direction that you wish to turn.

* For a quadcopter with three axes apply the yaw first and hold moving it towards the direction that you intend to turn. As the drone begins turning then slowly move your roll controls in the direction as the turn. The roll should be adjusted to compensate for the side-slip. For a perfect adjustment using a quadcopter with three axes requires time and practice, so don't expect to be able to do it flawlessly first time.

* To make more precise turns make sure you pull back a bit on the pitch but maintaining the control of the roll and yaw in the correct place.

How to do a Barrel Roll:

A barrel roll occurs when the drone performs an entire rotation around the roll axis, and then comes to stand upright. Make sure there's enough distance between the drone's axis and the ground prior to you try this technique. To do a barrel roll:

* Keep the throttle full until you have reached a certain level.

• Push the throttle to both sides of the throttle while pushing the throttle back to approximately 50 percent.

* Continue to keep the roll to the fullest until approximately half the roll has been completed.

* At the point that the drone is nearly upright again, press the full throttle once more to maintain the altitude and decrease the roll axis.

How to do a Backflip:

The drone can perform an incredibly quick backflip in mid-air. Here's the method:

* Take off with the throttle up to 20 feet from the ground.

* Now turn the right stick in the opposite direction, with a strong force.

* When the drone starts to turn, move the left stick towards the center to restore the balance.

For making it simpler to use, switch on Stability Mode right after the flip to ensure that the drone can be stabilized automatically.

Forward flips are accomplished in the same manner by flicking the stick on the right in the opposite direction, instead of going backwards.

How to make funnels:

The funnel appears to be the appearance of a nose-down turn down the drain. For a funnel to be constructed:

* Take your drone into the air.

The only thing you have to do is push forward to either the left or right, and then full push to pitch ahead.

* Use the throttle to maintain the altitude.

Advanced Techniques to master:

* Fly using a figure eight pattern.

* Do bank turns.

* Do a barrel roll.

* Do a backflip.

* Do funnels.

• Run an obstacle course.

Chapter 11: What Is A Drone?

Although the term "drone" has been used in mainstream media to refer to any aircraft that is unmanned but the precise technical name is "Unmanned Aerial Vehicle (UAV)'. The term "UAV" is a better word because it is wide enough to encompass all drones, from the tiny quadcopters we're all familiar with to more advanced drones for military use.

A Unmanned Aerial Vehicle is basically an aircraft that doesn't require a pilot to operate. UAVs typically include control systems to assist in adapting to changes in air flow and wind pressure. They also have remote systems that allow you to control them from a distance. The level of automation depends on the sophistication that the drone. There are certain types of UAVs which have been designed to carry out certain tasks with no human intervention while others require the complete attention of an on-ground controller.

Types of DRONES

The rapid growth of drone technology over the last couple of years has left us with an array of drones, making it difficult to classify them. We would however like to categorize them using some general categories that could aid in understanding the vast range of drones are on the market.

1. Classification based on Size
In accordance with size the drone is of three primary types of drones
Nano and Micro Drones

They are among the smallest drones on the market currently. They come in sizes that range in size from a tiny bug to around 50 centimeters long. They're quite an achievement of technological advancement. These drones feature sophisticated rotors that give high maneuverability, even in small areas. They are frequently employed to spy on people and to spread harmful biological viruses.

Mini drones

Mini drones are a bit bigger that Micro as well as Nano drones. They range between 50cm and 2 meters in size. Because of their small dimensions, they are mainly fixed-wing models, with a few models that have the rotary wings. They are typically launched to air with a manual launcher.

Medium drones

Medium drones are larger in weight and mass than small drones, but aren't as big or heavy as lighter aircraft. They can weigh up to 200kg. Hence, they typically are lifted up with the help of two to three persons before they glide by themselves.

Large drones

They are among the largest drones that are available. They're the size of piloted aircrafts and are frequently employed by the military to carry out extremely sensitive missions in the active zones of war and in regions with a high chance of loss. They are often used to conduct reconnaissance and can occasionally be employed for dropping explosives.

2. Classification based on Range

Drones are also classified based on their range, which basically means how far from their controllers drones can fly.

Drones with Very Close Range

Drones of this class can fly for between 30 and 45 minutes or one hour if powered by highly robust and efficient batteries. They can fly for just 5km. Therefore, they are mostly employed for leisure purposes.

Close Range Drones

Drones that are in this category are able to fly for up to six hours on a single charge. Additionally, they can fly for around 50 km. Hence they are usually used to conduct small surveillance.

Short Range Drones

Drones that are short-ranged can have the range of 50km up to 150km. They can fly for as long as 12 hours at a time. They are typically employed to monitor and for filmmaking.

Mid-Range Drones

These are more robust drones. They're fast drones and are able to fly up to 700km from the controller. They typically have extremely powerful batteries that allow drones keep flying for several days. They are typically employed for military surveillance as well as tracking weather patterns and geo-mapping.

3. Classification using the installed equipment

i. With Camera

Drones equipped with cameras have an impressive appeal for vloggers and film makers. With a camera installed you can utilize drones to capture stunning photos from some of the most amazing angles. Certain of these shots could have been nearly impossible to take decades ago, or required advanced equipment and an entire team of experts but now with a drone, you can lift it to the angle you desire and snap the picture. It will save you lots of time and money.

ii. With GPS

Drones that come with GPS are becoming more sought-after. With GPS in place, you will be able to stamp your videos according to the location in which they were taken. You can assign them tasks to specific locations and automatically return when having completed the assignment. They are also able to provide you with real-time location information in the field.

iii. With Stabilizer

The stabilizing element added to drones improves the capabilities of flight for the drone. By using gyroscopic technology the drone is more stable, making it much easier to control and perform more powerful motions in the air. It improves the navigation of drones and makes them better suited as a professional camera.

iv. With FPV

FPV is essentially a first-person view, meaning drones that are equipped with this feature are able to record events from the viewpoint of a viewer. FPV allows you to operate the drones from a distance by using portable monitors. They are frequently used for filmmaking and for shooting interviews.

4. Classification through the flight mechanism

Fixed Wing

Fixed-wing drones operate on the same principle of operation as an aircraft. They create lift due to the rapid and forward movement of the wing in the air. Because of their greater reach and longer fly-time they are often used for long-distance surveillance missions and geo-mapping, among others.

Benefits
I. Fixed-wing drones are able to stay on the ground for extremely long times for a long time
ii. They are able to fly that exceed 2500 km above the sea level

iii. They are able to carry larger payloads than drones with rotary wings.

iv. They are more thrust-based producing efficiency

V. They are able to cover a larger area simultaneously

Negatives

i. They can't be able to hover over an area while airborne

ii. A higher level of instruction is required to effectively manage them

iii. They are a lot harder to land since they usually require a parachute, runway, or a net to catch the aircraft after landing.

iv. They're a bit more expensive than rotary drones.

It is a. Because of the drone's inability to hover, making images using fixed-wing drones is a bit difficult. Many shots are likely to be captured and put together to create an acceptable image.

vi. Typically, fixed-wing planes will require launchers and runways to launch.

Single Rotor Drones

Single rotor drones are based on the principle of helicopters. They employ only one rotor for lift, and a tail rotor to regulate the direction of the drone and increase stability. It is crucial to keep in mind that single-rotor drones tend to be seldom employed.

Benefits

i. They can be powered by gasoline engines that can allow them to remain airborne for longer.

ii. They are able to hover vertically

iii. They can carry more payload than multi-rotors.

iv. They tend to be stronger and last longer

V. They have better thrust-generating capacity than multi-rotor drones.

Advantages

i. single-rotor drones are more expensive than multi-rotor drones.

ii. They are more difficult than multi-rotor drones. They are, however, more user-friendly than fixed-wing drones.

iii. They require a certain degree of proficiency to fly them

iv. Single rotor drones require additional precautions to be used because of the increased dangers associated with spinning blades

V. They need more frequent maintenance on their mechanical systems.

Multirotor Drones

Multirotor drones are among the most frequently used kind of drones. They are extensively employed to take aerial photos surveys, aerial photography and more. Multirotor drones make use of multiple rotating rotors to create lift. They are further classified according to their number of rotors they use. We have tricopters with three rotors. Quadcopters employ four, hexacopters have six and octocopters have eight rotors. In all of them quadcopters, quadcopters are the most frequently used.

Benefits

I. The multirotor drones can be less expensive

ii. They are very easy to control and require only a few hours of instruction

iii. They are the cheapest to fly since they do not require routine mechanical maintenance

iv. They are extremely solid

V. They are able to hover over a location in the air

Negatives

I. Multirotor drones are not able to remain in the air. They typically stay between 15 to 30 minutes

ii. They can't carry a huge payload

iii. They can't be used in long-distance surveillance applications.

iv. They are significantly slower than fixed wing drones.

V. It isn't very efficient with energy as it spends most of its energy to keep its air in a stable state.

5. Classification is based on Energy Source

There are a variety of energy sources which propel drones in the present. The choice of fuel source is largely dependent on the dimensions and function of drone. The most popular sources of energy are;

i. Battery-powered

Small drones are typically powered by rechargeable lithium polymer battery. They're suitable for lightweight drones that have a short range.

ii. Liquid fuel-powered

The larger drones, like those employed for military purposes are typically powered by the combustion of fuels like the kerosene.

These drones travel over long distances and are usually required to remain airborne for prolonged periods of time.

iii. Fuel cell-powered

The fuel cells transform chemical energy into electrical energy. They are highly eco-friendly and efficient, but they're quite heavy, so they are only suitable for larger drones that have long time to fly.

Applications and uses of DRONES

Drones are a great tool to serve a variety of applications.

I. Filming and aerial photography

Drones can capture aerial photos and film events from high angles which not so long back would require helicopters and a complete video crew. News reporters, both professional and amateur, have also begun to employ drones to record the happenings and events that can be at up to 500m distance from where they report. Drones are more frequently used to cover sporting events, such as The PGA championships, The US Open, and even The 2016 Rio Olympic Games. Professional sport teams are also using them for training purposes to give them an aerial view that provides more insights on tactics and positioning.

ii. Mapping

Drones offer a low-cost and effective method of recording an area. The aerial coverage derived from drones is used to make 3D model that accurately represent the area. Drones' ability to access areas that humans are unable to reach is what makes them ideal for mapping geographic areas. Mountain tops steep slopes, steep slopes and an erosion-prone shorelines are accessible and analysed in real-time,

iii. Rescue

The use of drones to rescue people is another popular use of drones. Drones are able to transport medical supplies, food items and other supplies quicker than human beings, especially in areas that have limited access. Depending on the size of the task drones may also be outfitted with infrared technologies that can assist in identifying heat-producing forms in the search for survivors following the aftermath of a major catastrophe.

Due to the effectiveness and growing potential of drones for search-and-rescue activities Many governments across the globe are investing hugely in the development the drone's technology within this field.

iv. Agriculture

Drones have been widely adopted by farmers to help them in their daily work because of the huge advantages they bring. Drones are a less expensive and more efficient means farmers can monitor their crops to check for irrigation problems, examine the health of their crops, monitor the rate of growth of the crops, and also to monitor the farm for intruders. The latest research is also being conducted to determine how drones can be utilized to mass plant and spray the crops using insecticides.

v. Surveillance

Drones can be utilized to monitor and secure areas because they cover a larger area in the most precise manner and at a greater speed than human security personnel are able to. By utilizing infrared technology as well as advanced software for facial recognition drones are able for surveillance of large events in order to be on the lookout for individuals and threats.

Drones can also be used for border security since they are able to cover and monitor large areas at the same time. Recently, the Estonian government Estonia purchased a collection of sophisticated drones to assist in monitoring the borders of Estonia.

Drones can also be utilized to observe wildfires, and provide fire departments with information in real-time regarding the extent of the fire, without placing anyone at risk.

vi. Monitoring wildlife

Poaching is a serious issue which is being faced by every region around the globe. Many reports continue to reveal the declining numbers of the rhino and elephant populations because they are frequently killed for their horns that are sold for huge sums. Although a variety of technological advances have been developed to reduce this issue and drones have proven as the most efficient. They are able to cover greater areas and work during the night by using infrared technology.

Apart from fighting poaching, conservationists have utilized drones to keep an eye on population. The tracking of animal populations is now a lot simpler quicker, less costly and more efficient by using drones. They provide a non-invasive method to track the animals.

vii. Environmental monitoring

Environmental organizations and non-governmental organizations across the globe are also experimenting with drones to monitor and safeguard the environment. They are commonly employed to monitor deforestation and to conduct critical studies and to analyze predictively volcanic craters, assess the quality of air at various temperatures, and keep in mind the changes in the rivers' flow and look for erosion issues.

viii. Exploration of minerals

Drones are being utilized for exploration of minerals, particularly the exploration of oil and natural gas. They are a cost-effective efficient, faster and less invasive method to determine the presence of precious minerals within the earth. Explorers are now able detect the structural pathways in mineralized fluids and gather more information without placing themselves in danger. Drones are also utilized to collect data that will be used to accurately estimate the volume of quarrying and extraction.

ix. Recreation

Drones are now increasingly being used to play with. With the increasing development of light-weight, low-cost drones, users can easily buy drones and enjoy some amusement using drones. Children can are able to play with them in their homes or go into parks to have amusement. However, the incessant use of drones has forced governments around the globe to set strict guidelines for using drones in recreational for recreational purposes.

x. Delivery

Although they are still severely limited by the FAA Some companies such as Amazon or Domino's Pizza have successfully delivered packages to customers by drones. These tests are considered to be an excellent evidence of concept, and it's just an issue of time before regulations become more relaxed and are accepted by more people.

xi. Inspection

The construction industry is also starting using drones for rigorous inspections of projects that could previously put people in danger. Drones can be utilized to monitor the development of a project, as well as to verify the strength of the structure of a building.

In addition to inspecting buildings that are under construction, drones also have been used to examine thoroughly solar panels, windmills and turbines cell towers pipelines and power lines. Drones are able to go where humans cannot and do so in a shorter amount of time and cost-effectively.

xii. Military

Drones were first created and built to be used in military operations. They've been employed for military use from the time of the first world. They offer a distinct advantage because they can be used in areas in which the risk of human casualties was high. They also helped to reduce casualties in war. But, as time went on drones began to be employed for much more than just dropping bombs. they were employed for high-altitude surveillance that produced vital intelligence. Drones also are utilized to find bombs because they can penetrate tiny areas and send feeds from cameras to the controllers located miles away.

www.ingramcontent.com/pod-product-compliance
Lightning Source LLC
Chambersburg PA
CBHW062117040426
42336CB00041B/1244